D1062309

Marylanders in Blue
The Artillery
and
The Cavalry

Daniel Carroll Toomey
&
Charles Albert Earp

Toomey Press
Baltimore, Maryland

3 1267 13261 5582

For information about this and other titles, contact

Toomey Press
P.O. Box 122
Linthicum, MD 21090
410-766-1211

Photographic Credits:
    D.C.T. – Daniel Carroll Toomey
    All others indicated by specific source

Book Design and Production:
    Cynthia Merrifield
    Merrifield Graphics & Publishing Service, Inc.
    Baltimore, Maryland

Printing:
    H.G. Roebuck & Son, Inc.
    Baltimore, Maryland

Library of Congress Card Number 99-070879
ISBN 06-9612670-8-9

Copyright © 1999 Toomey Press
All Rights Reserved
Printed in the United States of America

PREFACE

On the eve of the Civil War the Regular Army of the United States Government numbered only 16,367 men. The Navy and Marine Corps totaled about 9,150. This slim force of professionals was supported by a state militia system ranging widely in organization, equipment, and competence. Before John Brown's Raid on Harper's Ferry in 1859, the State of Maryland had not responded to a military crises since the war with Mexico in 1846.

With the out break of war in April of 1861 the Federal Government attempted to create a 75,000 man army overnight that would be able to defend the country, suppress the rebellion, and turn in its equipment by the end of the soldiers ninety-day enlistment. This we know, for both the North and the South, was impossible.

During the course of the war the State of Maryland mustered thirty-five regiments, batteries, and independent companies into the Union Army. Six additional regiments of United States Colored troops and nearly 4,000 Navy and Marine Corps personal were also credited to the states quotas. Fourteen native sons rose from the ranks of the Regular Army or the United States Volunteers to ware the stars of a general in the Union Army. Only one, Louis M. Goldsborough, achieved the rank of Rear Admiral. Seventeen others wore a badge of even greater distinction, the Medal of Honor.

In the peaceful years that followed the war Maryland's blue clad soldiers returned to civilian life. They celebrated their victories in over fifty posts of the Grand Army of the Republic and remembered their fallen comrades on Memorial Day. With the exception of a few monuments scattered across battlefields and cemeteries, it is not too far from the truth to say that for the Maryland Volunteers their history died with them. Not since the publication of Frederick Wild's history of Alexander's Battery in 1912 has a book been written solely about those Marylanders who chose to defend the Union during the War of the Rebellion.

Who then were the Marylanders in Blue? What was their contribution to the Union war effort? Despite the fact that Maryland remained in the Union; that it contributed more white soldiers (46,672) than New Hampshire or Vermont; and more black solders (23,763) than any Boarder or Northern state except Kentucky, little has been written about these patriots of 1861 who were often forced to chose between flag and family when the time came to enlist.

Marylanders in Blue, The Artillery and The Cavalry is the first of a projected multi volume study that will cover each branch of the service and unit raised in the state during the Civil War. Where possible, photographs of soldiers who actually served in these units as well as their weapons and equipment have been included. Collectively they will present the faces, relics, and history of the Maryland Volunteers of 1861–1865.

In preparing this project Charles Earp and I would like to thank a number of people who responded willingly to our many request and made helpful suggestions that improved our final text. They are Jay A. Graybeal, Director, Historical Society of Carroll County, R. J. Rockerfeller, Maryland State Archives, Jennifer Tolpa of the Massachusetts Historical Society, Ann Sindelar, Western Reserve Historical Society, Ted Alexander and Paul Chiles of the Antietam National Battlefield. We would also like to extend our appreciation to Mr. and Mrs. Walter R. Harding, Jr. and Mr. Gil Barrett for allowing us to use photographs from their private collections.

Daniel Carroll Toomey   Charles Albert Earp

Contents

VOLUNTEERS WANTED!

PEOPLE OF DORCHESTER COUNTY,

Our State has been invaded, and ten thousand men have been called for from this State, to aid in driving back the invaders. Patriotism and duty calls upon us to join our fellow citizens of Pennsylvania and the Western Shore of Maryland in defence of their homes.

I am old, but am ready to give my few remaining days to aid in the defence of our State, and in putting down this unholy rebellion. Volunteers are wanted for a short time; one or more Companies. All who are willing to go with me are requested to report to me, or in my absence to JOHN T. JACKSON, Esq., office of the Register of Wills.

Do not delay, come at once, every hour is valuable; I will go with you wherever you may be sent, and remain with you so long as our services may be needed.

THOMAS H. HICKS.

Cambridge, Md., June 18, 1863.

PRINTED AT THE "HERALD OFFICE," CAMBRIDGE, MD.

Recruiting poster for Dorchester County: During the summer of 1863 Lee's Army of Northern Virginia crossed the Potomac River for a second invasion of the North which ultimately ended at the Battle of Gettysburg. President Lincoln ordered a general call up of militia in the affected states. The term of service for these emergency troops was six months. Thomas Holiday Hicks, Maryland's first wartime governor, lent his name to the recruiting drive on the Eastern Shore. The engraved eagle makes this an extremely fine example of a Civil War broadside. (D.C.T.)

MOBILIZATION

Following the bombardment of Fort Sumter, the Sixth Massachusetts Infantry Regiment was attacked as it passed through Baltimore City en route to the Nation's Capital. Many Marylanders wished to preserve the Union but could not condone an attack on the Southern states. Bonds were especially close with Virginia, which had just joined the Confederacy. Governor Thomas Holiday Hicks wrote a letter to President Lincoln requesting that the state's allotment of four regiments from the first call for volunteers not be enforced, as recruiting at this time would only strengthen the hand of secessionist in the state. For this reason no three month regiments were raised in the spring of 1861. Those citizens who were eager to "join up" were forced to go to Delaware, Pennsylvania or Washington, D.C. to do so.[1]

A second call for volunteers was issued in May of 1861 to serve for three years. Maryland's quota was 15,578 of which 9,355 were furnished. The men that enlisted during the latter part of 1861 and the first half of 1862 did so before the advent of the draft or bounty payments. They formed the backbone of the state's three year regiments, served the longest in the field and suffered the greatest number of casualties among the Maryland Volunteers.

Recruiting during the Civil War was not a well planned event. Rather than enlist men en masse and then assign them to sequentially numbered units, the companies, batteries, and regiments were recruited simultaneously and in competition with each other. Without a sufficient number of men a regiment could not be mustered into federal service. Thus, many of the Maryland regiments did not take the field until 1862.

As the war progressed the Federal Government levied more and more demands on the loyal states for enlistments. Maryland, with a significant number of its war aged citizens serving in the Confederate Army (10,000–15,000), was hard pressed to fill its quotas. Others were exempt due to employment by one of the four major railroads in the state or various protected occupations. It must also be noted that a large percentage of the general population was indifferent or outright hostile to the Federal Government. When the Draft was finally enacted in August of 1862 these feelings were manifested in different ways. Drafted men could purchase a substitute for $300 to $700. They could pay a commutation fee of $300—which was only good until the next draft. This practice was not unique to Maryland. Nationally, 86,724 drafted men paid a commutation fee during the war. Finally, they could secure employment in an exempt position.[2]

LINCOLN'S CALL FOR VOLUNTEER'S 1861-1865

Date	National	Maryland	Supplied	Commutations
Apr. 15, 1861	75,000	3,123	0	0
May 3, 1861	500,000	15,578	9,355	0
Jul. 12, 1862	300,000	8,532	(total with Aug. 4)	0
Aug. 4, 1862	300,000	8,532	3,586	0
Jun. 15, 1863	Militia*	10,000	1,615	0
Oct. 17, 1863	500,000	10,794	6,244	1,106
Mar. 14, 1864	200,000	4,317	9,365	2,528
Mar. 14, 1864	Militia*	2,000	1,297	
Jul. 18, 1864	500,000	10,947	10,266	31
Dec. 19, 1864	300,000	9,142	4,944	3
Totals:	2,675,000	70,965	46,672	3,666

* A general call up of militia in states affected by the Gettysburg and Monocacy campaigns.[3]

To *Henry Wilson*

You are hereby notified that you have been Drafted into the Militia Forces of the United States, in the State of Maryland, under the Act of Congress, of July 1862, in *Harford* County, as part of the Quota of said County; and you are further notified to appear on *Tuesday* the *21st* day of *October*, 1862, at *Havre de Grace* in said County, to be there provided with transportation to *Baltimore* the place of Rendezvous for the Drafted Militia of said County.

Edwd. A. Hall — Commissioner to Superintend the Enrollment and Draft of the Militia for *Harford* County.

Bel. Air, Oct. 15 1862.

Draft Notice for 1862: Each county and Baltimore City constituted an Enrollment District. Edward A. Hall was the commissioner for Harford County and signed this simple but effective notice. Henry Wilson of Magnolia was ordered to report on Tuesday, October 21, 1862, at Havre de Grace where transportation to Baltimore City would be provided. (D.C.T.)

To manage Maryland's mobilization effort John A. J. Creswell of Cecil County was appointed Assistant Adjutant General and Superintendent of Enrollment. Each county and Baltimore City constituted one Enrollment District with an officer in charge of each district. After the enrollments were completed and legal exemptions deleted, the state's quota was drawn by ballet from the remaining names.

Governor Augustus W. Bradford was very active in the recruiting process and highly supportive of the troops in the field. He appointed John Pendleton Kennedy to head a committee of fifty prominent citizens to aid in the recruitment of Maryland soldiers. He also met with the Union League and the Union City Convention to find ways to increase enlistments. During the summer of 1863 Lee launched his second invasion of the North. Ex-Governor Thomas Holiday Hicks lent his name to the recruiting of emergency troops in Dorchester County.[4]

As an inducement to enlist prior to the draft, the Federal Government offered bounty money that was soon added to by state and even some local jurisdictions. These sums are even more impressive when compared to the meager $13.00 a month a drafted soldier would receive.

John Andrew Jackson Creswell: An officer in the state militia and member of the House of Delegates, he was appointed Assistant Adjutant General and Superintendent of Enrollment. (D.C.T.)

In 1863 a recruiting advertisement for Alexander's Baltimore Light Artillery explained the complicated, but profitable, gain for all who enlisted before July 10. A Federal bounty of $402.00 would be paid as follows: At the time of muster $27.00; two months after muster $50.00; and $50.00 every six months after that until his three year enlistment was completed at which time he would receive a final payment of $75.00. To this was added an additional bounty of $100.00 by Baltimore City bringing the grand total to $502.00.[5]

As the war entered its third year the original terms of enlistment began to expire. The Union war effort would be sadly diminished if its most experienced regiments suddenly left

State of Maryland Bounty Certificate.

Office of County Commissioners for *Washington* County, **and.**

CASH $150 PAID.
CERTIFICATE FOR $100.

May 14ᵗʰ 1864.

This Certificate entitles *Archibald Colbert* of Company *G. Coles Regiment Md. Vol. Cavalry* to One Hundred Dollars, payable in *five* monthly instalments of twenty dollars each, from the *25ᵗʰ* day of *Feby* *1864* being the date of his muster.

(A further sum of $ *50* will be paid BY THE STATE, under the provisions of its Bounty Act at the expiration of his term of service, or when honorably discharged therefrom.)

Jno L. Smith, Clerk County Commissioners.

1st Instalment, paid *14ᵗʰ* day of *May* 1864. *J. A. McCoul*
2d Instalment, paid *14ᵗʰ* day of *May* " *J. A. McCoul*
3d Instalment, paid *11ᵗʰ* day of *Aug* "
4th Instalment, paid *11ᵗʰ* day of *Aug* " *Jno L. Smith clk*
5th Instalment, paid *11ᵗʰ* day of *Aug* "

by reason of *G. O. No 53 Mid Mil Div U.S. 1865*

No objection to his being re-enlisted is known to exist.*

Said *Arch Colbert* was born in *Washington County* in the State of *Maryland* is *Thirty Two* years of age, *five* feet *three* inches high, *Florid* complexion, *Blue* eyes, *Dark* hair, and by occupation, when enrolled, a *Laborer*

Given at *Harpersferry Va* this *Twenty Eighth* day of *June 1865*

State Bounty Certificate: Record of payment to Private Arch Colbert, Company M, First Potomac Home Brigade Cavalry. Colbert was to receive $20.00 a month for five months after his enlistment on February 25, 1864, and an additional $50.00 when discharged. When actively campaigning, pay schedules were seldom met. Colbert's installments were lumped together in May and August of 1864. (D.C.T.)

the field on the eve of what everyone hoped would be the final campaign season. To keep this from becoming a reality soldiers were offered strong inducements to reenlist: a $400.00 bounty, a 30 day furlough, and the title of Veteran Volunteer for himself and his regiment if a sufficient number of men agreed to serve for three more years or the end of the war. Most of the Maryland regiments that were formed early in the war agreed to "see it through" and finished the war in the field. Their triumphant return was bittersweet after the assassination of Abraham Lincoln in April of 1865.[6]

Notes

1. Charles B. Clark, "Recruitment of Union Troops in Maryland, 1861-1865," *Maryland Historical Magazine*, Vol. 53, No. 2, June 1958, pp. 153-154.
2. *Historical Times Illustrated Encyclopedia of the Civil War*, (New York: 1986), Patricia L. Faust, ed., pp. 155-156; Clark, p. 159.
3. Clark, p. 173
4. Henry F. Powell, *Tercentenary History of Maryland*, (Chicago – Baltimore: 1925), Vol. IV, pp. 25-26; Clark, p. 159; J Thomas Scharf, *The Chronicles of Baltimore*, (Baltimore, 1874), pp. 591-592.
5. *The Baltimore American and Commercial Advertizer*, July 4, 1863.
6. Francis A. Lord, *They Fought for the Union*, (New York: 1960), pp. 12-13.

THE ARTILLERY

BY

CHARLES ALBERT EARP

Dedicated to the memory of my ancestor,
Sergeant Charles T. Marsden,
Battery A, First Maryland Light Artillery,
United States Volunteers,
killed in the battle of Antietam, Maryland,
September 17, 1862.

CONTENTS

CIVIL WAR LIGHT ARTILLERY

All but one of the batteries raised by the state of Maryland for the Federal army were highly mobile horse drawn units known as light or field artillery. Each battery carried a state designation, such as Battery A, First Maryland Light Artillery. It was also referred to by the name of its commander, such as Walcott's Battery. Thus, most batteries carried a dual identity.

Although there were a variety of field guns used during the war, including some of foreign manufacture, the two that were the most popular in both the Union and Confederate armies, were the Napoleon and the Ordnance gun. The Napoleon, usually a 12 pounder, was a smooth bore, muzzle-loading gun or howitzer made of bronze. The Ordnance gun was a rifled muzzle loader of iron or steel also called a three-inch rifle because of the diameter of the ammunition it used. The latter was the more accurate while the Napoleon was better for closer work. A Maryland artilleryman recalled that in target practice their smooth bore gun hit the target, an oak tree, one time out of four and the solid shot bounced off. The Ordnance gun scored the first time and buried the shot deep in the trunk.

He also tells that their Ordnance gun at the battle of Monocacy put three shells into a barn sheltering sharp shooters a half mile away and set it on fire.

Effective range varied with the target, type of gun, and the gunner's ability to see the fall of his shot and make necessary corrections. Practical range varied from 1,500 to 2,000 yards. To the extent that the records reveal, all of the Maryland Light Artillery Batteries in the field consisted of Ordnance guns.[1]

Ammunition was of many varieties but could be categorized as solid shot, shell, case, and canister, each being used for a different tactical purpose. A solid shot was most accurate and had the longest range of the four types. Shell, hollowed and filled with powder, was fused and exploded into large pieces. Case, also called shrapnel, was similar to shell but also contained many musket balls, which flew in all directions when the projectile exploded. Canister was a tin can filled with walnut sized iron balls packed in sawdust, which made the cannon a giant shotgun. It was best used in a smooth bored field piece and was deadly at close range.[2]

A battery usually consisted of six guns, sometimes less, rarely more. Its equipment, in addition to the guns, included limbers, caissons, a forge, and a battery wagon. Supporting each gun was a limber to pull it and another limber drawing a caisson. A limber was a two-wheeled cart carrying an ammunition chest drawn by a team of horses, usually six in number but sometimes four. In transit, the gun, also mounted on a two-wheeled carriage, was hooked to the back of the limber. A caisson, which supported each gun, was a two-wheeled cart carrying two ammunition chests, a spare wheel and various tools. A limber pulled by four or six horses also drew it. Supporting the entire battery was a forge and battery wagon. The forge was a complete, mobile blacksmith's shop and carried enough spare parts to completely rebuild a gun carriage. These valuable mobile workshops were normally held in the rear of the army and did not go into battle with the guns of the battery. The battery's equipment also included six more caissons, which contained the ammunition reserve.[3]

The ammunition chest for a twelve pounder Napoleon contained 32 rounds of ammunition. A fully loaded platoon (gun, limbers, and caisson) carried 128 rounds of ammunition. The total weight of a fully equipped gun and limber was about 3,800 pounds.[4]

Typical four gun Union battery: This photograph shows a line of cannons with their supporting limbers and caissons. The battery commander stands proudly in front of the formation. Note the mobile forage in the far right background and the extra wheel on the rear of each caisson. (*Millers Photographic History*)

A six gun battery was commanded by a captain and consisted of three sections of two guns each, commanded by lieutenants. A lieutenant also was in command of the line of reserve caissons. A platoon, consisting of a gun and its supporting equipment, was in charge of a sergeant, called the "Chief of Piece." Two corporals assisted him, one in charge of the gun, the other the caisson. Three riders, known as the lead, swing and wheel drivers respectively, rode the left horse of each pair and drove the six horse teams that drew the gun and its limber or the caisson and its limber.[5]

The gun crew consisted of nine men who were positioned two at the gun's muzzle, two at the gun's breech, three at the limber and one (a corporal) at the caisson. The ninth man, a corporal, was positioned at the trail of the gun, aimed it, and directed its crew. The battery's other personnel consisted of a quartermaster sergeant, an orderly sergeant, five artificers (two blacksmiths, a carpenter/wheelwright and a leather worker), two buglers and the bearer of the battery flag called a guidon. The typical size of a battery was about 123 men and 146 horses.[6]

The officers, sergeants, buglers and guidon bearer were mounted; the canoneers normally walked so as not to wear out the horses with their additional weight. If they rode on the limbers and caissons it was a rugged and dangerous ride. Roads usually were dirt, rutted and pot holed and were quagmires in bad weather. In addition, the battery often had to ford streams and traverse open country. The riders could be badly shaken up or suffer serious falls. On top of all that they were sitting on live ammunition.[7]

Each member of the gun's crew had a specific, repetitive task to perform, much like today's assembly line worker, but was able to do all other tasks as battle conditions sometimes necessitate. The officers and sergeants carried side arms but the gun crews and drivers were armed only with sabers.[8]

A battery's position in action varied with the terrain and tactical considerations, but regulations called for 14 yards between guns. Allowing 2 yards for the gun itself, the battery extended over a distance of 82 yards from right to left. The limbers were positioned 6 yards behind the guns and the caisson 11 yards behind the limbers. The depth of the battery position was 47 yards. Normally the teams remained hitched to their vehicles, but when a position seemed relatively permanent, they were unhitched and taken to the rear to a place of comparative safety.[9]

A battery generally maneuvered at a trot and did not gallop except in cases of extreme emergency. A well-trained gun crew could deploy for action and fire one round in twenty-five seconds. The maximum rate of fire was two to four rounds per minute. However, the normal rate of fire was one round every two to three minutes. Civil War guns had no recoil devices and, when fired, rolled back a considerable distance and had to be pushed back into position and re-aimed after each firing. The sighting and range finding equipment of the time left much to be desired. Such accuracy as existed, depended largely on the experience and skill of the corporal who aimed the gun. It was the aiming rather than the loading, which took the time.[10]

Gun crews, riders and horses were often subjected to devastating counter battery fire and rifle fire, especially from sharp shooters. When preparing for action, as time allowed, the battery sought what natural protection it could or threw up gun emplacements of dirt, logs or whatever material was available. Because of the vulnerability of its personnel, an infantry unit was usually assigned to protect a battery in action.[11]

Three of the Maryland batteries saw active service with the Army of the Potomac and other commands. Three others served in the defenses of Baltimore and Washington. Only one company of the seventh, a heavy artillery unit, was actually organized and it, too, was on duty in the defenses of Baltimore.

THE GIST
ARTILLERY
BATTALION
UNITED STATES
VOLUNTEERS

W hen President Lincoln called for volunteers at the beginning of the Civil War, numerous individuals prominent in politics, business and society, answered the call and used their position and influences to raise military units. One such was William H. Purnell, former Deputy Attorney General and Comptroller of the state of Maryland. He was appointed Postmaster of Baltimore by the Lincoln administration in 1861. Purnell was responsible for the recruitment, organization and training of a unit known as the Purnell Legion. It consisted of one infantry regiment, two batteries of light artillery, and three companies of cavalry.[1]

The two batteries, designated Battery A and Battery B, First Maryland Light Artillery, United States Volunteers, comprised a battalion commanded by Major Edward R. Petherbridge. The Purnell Legion, including the two batteries, was recruited and trained during the summer and fall of 1861 and was assigned to the Middle Department, commanded by General John A. Dix, with headquarters in Baltimore. The battalion was called the Gist Artillery in honor of General Mordecai Gist who was a Maryland Revolutionary War hero.[2]

The Purnell Legion experienced its first field service in late 1861 when, with other troops from the Baltimore command, it participated in an expedition to the Delmarva Peninsula. The Delmarva Peninsula consists of the southern part of Delaware, the Maryland counties east of the Chesapeake Bay, and the Virginia counties of Accomac and Northampton, which are the only Virginia counties separated from the rest of the state by water. Several camps of rendezvous were established in Accomac and Northampton counties to raise military units for the Confederacy. An estimated 1,000 men were under arms plus 1,500 to 2,000 militia which could be called into service. All commercial and business connections, as well as transportation to the North had been severed; the postal service had ceased and the lighthouse at Cape Charles was out of service.

The administration hoped to save these two counties for the union, peacefully if possible, by force if necessary. To this end a force of some 3,500 men was assembled on Maryland's eastern shore under the command of Brigadier General Henry Lockwood.[3]

Among the units stationed in Baltimore who participated in the expedition was the Second Massachusetts Light Artillery, known as Nims' Battery, two officers of which transferred to the Gist Artillery. John W. Wolcott became Captain of Battery A and John Bigelow became adjutant of the battalion.[4]

General Lockwood's mission was to disburse the Virginia Confederate forces, disarm any militia companies in adjacent Maryland counties hostile to the Federal government, and stem the flow of material and information moving across the Chesapeake Bay. The mission was completed without any actual combat taking place. The Purnell Legion batteries were stationed at various locations on the peninsula in Maryland and Virginia from November of 1861 to May of 1862. Principally, these were in Drummondtown and Eastville, the county seats of the two Virginia counties. This gave the batteries some experience in the field before being transferred to the Army of the Potomac.[5]

Lieutenant James H. Rigby, of Battery A, wrote his parents in November, 1861 from Berlin in Worcester County, Maryland:

"The people of the place were very glad to see us… We were greeted with cheers by the men and the waving of handkerchiefs by the ladies. They gave us a very bountiful collation of Hot coffee and Hot biscuits, which was very refreshing to men who had fasted for 18 hours…They have furnished us with straw for our tents, and are furnishing us rations, free gratis."[6]

Colonel Purnell resigned his commission in February, 1862. General Dix, in approving the resignation, noted "Colonel Purnell is the Post Master of the City of Baltimore and can not perform the duties of both offices." With his resignation the Purnell Legion ceased to exist as a single command although its individual units retained the Legion's name for the remainder of their enlistment.[7]

Major Petherbridge, believing the battalion would be dissolved, also resigned; and General Lockwood, who did not approve of the legion concept, recommended that he not be replaced. However, the battalion was continued by the War Department and the major withdrew his resignation, serving in the Army of the Potomac until July, 1862.

Major General Henry J. Hunt, Commander of the artillery reserve of the Army of the Potomac, twice refers to it in his correspondence as Petherbridge's artillery brigade, although it was a battalion. Major Petherbridge again resigned July 15, 1862, after the battle of Malvern Hill, at which time the battalion organization was discontinued.[8]

A bookbinder by trade, Petherbridge had served in the Mexican War as 1st Sergeant in Tilghman's Light Artillery Battery of Maryland and District of Columbia Volunteers. In 1851, he was appointed agent to receive all State owned arms and equipment from the various militia units. After his resignation from the Gist Artillery, Petherbridge was among a group of citizens who sponsored an invitation to join an independent military organization, to be known as the Maryland Line, for the defense of the city during the Confederate invasion of Maryland in September, 1862. He also saw brief service as commander of volunteer cavalry during the Confederate raid on Baltimore in July, 1864. He died in 1891 and is buried in Green Mount Cemetery in Baltimore.[9]

Lieutenant John Bigelow, Adjutant of the Gist Artillery Battalion, left

Harvard in his senior year to enlist as a private in the Second Massachusetts Light Artillery. He soon advanced to the rank of lieutenant. When the battery was stationed in Maryland he transferred to the Gist Artillery Battalion as Adjutant. While serving temporarily on the staff of General Lockwood, Bigelow procured plans of the defenses of Norfolk, Virginia, which aided in the subsequent capture of that city.

He was wounded in the battle of Malvern Hill but returned to duty in time for the battle of Fredericksburg in December of 1862. He resigned the same month to become Captain of the Ninth Massachusetts Light Artillery. At Gettysburg he fought his battery with great distinction and was wounded again during Hood's assault on the second day. After recovering from his wound Captain Bigelow rejoined his battery and participated in all the battles of the Army of the Potomac through the siege of Petersburg. In December of 1864, he commanded an artillery battalion but was forced to resign due to disability with the rank of Brevet Major.[10]

The Gist Artillery retained its battalion organization from the time it joined the Army of the Potomac until the end of the Peninsula Campaign in July, 1862. However, Battery A and B did not serve together. As part of the army's artillery reserve during that campaign they were assigned independently to support various infantry units. In the major reorganization of the army which followed, they were attached to different infantry divisions as part of the divisional artillery. Their separate histories follow.

BATTERY A FIRST MARYLAND LIGHT ARTILLERY UNITED STATES VOLUNTEERS

Battery A, First Maryland Light Artillery, United States Volunteers, was organized and mustered in at Baltimore and Pikesville, Maryland, in August and September, 1861, as part of the Purnell Legion. Its first captain was John W. Wolcott who served in that capacity until he resigned in December of 1862. He was succeeded as captain by First Lieutenant James H. Rigby who continued in command until the end of the war.[1]

The battery was initially part of the command of General John A. Dix in Baltimore and then was sent to the Eastern Shore of Maryland where it took part in the operations against Confederate forces in the two Virginia counties south of the Maryland state line.[2]

In May of 1862 Battery A, generally know as Wolcott's Battery, joined the Army of the Potomac during the Peninsula Campaign against Richmond and was assigned to the Artillery Reserve of General Fitz-John Porter's Fifth Corps. It participated in all the campaigns of that army until March 1864. During General George B. McClellan's change of base and retreat down the peninsula after the battle of Seven Pines, the battery defended the bridges at various river crossings. On June 26, 1862, during the battle of Mechanicsville, four guns under command of Lieutenant Rigby were stationed at Grapevine Bridge. Two days later, the guidon bearer, Private Ridgeley, was wounded in action at Woodbury Bridge on the Chickahominy. The battery was at Woodbury Bridge on June 29 and White Oak Swamp Bridge on June 30, arriving at Malvern Hill about 3 P.M. that day. At Malvern Hill the final battle of the Peninsula Campaign was fought and involved one of the greatest concentration of massed artillery during the war.[3]

On the morning of July 1, Battery A was subjected to heavy artillery fire for over two hours until it moved to a less exposed position. The Sixteenth Michigan Infantry supported the battery during this period, helped carry ammunition and supplied replacements for two men in the second section who had been wounded. About 3 P.M., the battery was ordered to the right of General Edwin V. Sumner's line to enfilade two Confederate batteries at a range of 1,600 yards. It remained in action at this site for about four hours until its ammunition was exhausted. Losses in the campaign were three wounded and one missing.[4]

Battery A did not participate in the battle of Second Bull Run, August 29-30, 1862, although the Fifth Corps was on the field. However, during the retreat of General John Pope's army toward Washington, there is evidence that Battery A was briefly engaged with Confederate artillery. Battery E, Second United States Artillery, was confronting Confederate gunners on Cub Run on August 31 and its commander noted in his report that "…a section of Captain Wolcott's Maryland Battery arriving, the enemy's guns were silenced." The battle credits of Battery A, inscribed on Captain Rigby's gravestone, includes Second Bull Run.[5]

The reports of Captain Wolcott and his superior, the division artillery chief, have not survived for the Antietam campaign of September 1862. However, there are references to the battery in other reports and particularly in a letter written by then Lieutenant Rigby immediately following the battle of Antietam.

After the Second Bull Run Campaign, the battery moved across the Potomac River and through Maryland to the village of Burkittsville, just below Crampton's Gap in South Mountain. Northwest of the mountains General Lee had divided his forces. General Jackson was investing Harper's Ferry and would force the surrender of the Federal garrison there. General Longstreet

Captain James H. Rigby: A native of Baltimore City, Rigby was a member of the Eagle Artillery before the war. He enlisted in August of 1861 as a first lieutenant and was promoted to captain of the battery on January 10, 1863. Captain Rigby died in 1889 and is buried in the Old National Cemetery in Baltimore. (Union Room Collection – MNGMHS)

was in the vicinity of Hagerstown. Some Confederate units had been posted in the mountain gaps to delay the Army of the Potomac approaching from the direction of Washington until the separated Confederate elements could concentrate for their advance into Pennsylvania. The actions at the three gaps, Crampton's, Fox's and Turner's, are known collectively as the battle of South Mountain; and it was the task of General William B. Franklin's Sixth Corps, to which Battery A now belonged, to clear Crampton's Gap.

The battery had reached a point four miles from the gap at about 2 P.M. on September 14, 1862. Skirmishers were deployed, followed by Battery A, and two infantry brigades. Contact was quickly made with the Confederates. The gap rose 600 feet above the valley and the mountain was heavily wooded. Approximately ten pieces of Confederate artillery opened fire from the woods and Battery A returned their fire. When the Union infantry attack began at the base of the mountain, it was necessary for the battery to change its position to support it. Lieutenant Rigby, described the movement vividly in a letter written five days later.

"We had to take the road through the village, which was being shelled by three 12 pounders posted on the mountain. From where we started, to the village, was about one mile and the position we were about to take, about one mile from the village; as soon as we appeared on the road, the Rebels turned their guns upon us, and such a shower of shot and shell as fell around us is not easily imagined...we went through at a full gallop...without a scratch and took our position. At dusk the Gap was in our possession with two Rebel guns and 500 prisoners."[6]

The Sixth Corps then proceed to Sharpsburg, Maryland, where on September 17, the battle of Antietam took place. Arriving on the field about noon, Battery A was posted near the Dunker Church not far from the center of the Federal line.

Posted directly to the right of Battery A, with its 8 three inch rifled cannons, was Battery B (Snow's) with six more, for a total of fourteen Maryland guns. By this time the main infantry action had shifted southward, but both batteries proceeded to exchange fire with the Confederate guns across the Hagerstown Pike in the West Woods.[7]

Horrified by what he saw on taking his position, Lieutenant Rigby wrote:

> "We were ordered into position in a field, from which the rebels had been driven in the morning; it was covered with dead and dying, so much so, that we could not get into position without striking them with our wheels. The crying of the wounded for water, the shrieks of the dying, mingled with the screeching of the shells, made up a scene so truly appalling and horrible, that I hoped to God, that I might never witness such another;
>
> But not so, after we shelled the woods opposite us and [had] driven two rebel batteries off, we were ordered to relieve a regular battery, about one thousand yards on our left and front. The Rebels were throwing shell and case into them like hail. We took their position and remained on the field until dark."[8]

This movement from the original position was into Mumma's swale where, while shelling the Confederate guns beyond the village of Sharpsburg, the battery sustained heavy casualties from sharpshooters on the Piper farm. Captain Wolcott complained vigorously to his artillery chief, Captain Emory Upton, and to Colonel William H. Irwin, commanding the nearest brigade. As a consequence of his protests, the Seventh Maine Infantry, under the command of Major Thomas W. Hyde, was detailed to advance and clear out the sharpshooters, which it did with considerable loss. It was not until nightfall that the fighting ceased.[9]

An artilleryman wrote home to his brother: "[Wolcott's] men fought like tigers and Wolcott showed himself to be a brave man. He took hold and helped work the guns himself and at one time there was only himself and three drivers to work one of them. The sharpshooters picked his men off. At one gun ten men were disabled." General Henry W. Slocum, the Division Commander wrote in his report: "…the artillery of the division… was well served and did good execution… the batteries of Captain Wolcott [and others] were all engaged and their fire proved very active and effective, twice silencing the enemy's and holding in check a large force of his infantry."[10]

Pvt. Charles C. Wintling: Enlisted in Rigby's Battery January 18, 1862, and served as a Veteran Volunteer until July 3, 1865. (Gil Barrett)

The battery's losses at Antietam were the heaviest it suffered in any campaign during the war. Sergeant Charles T. Marsden [the author's ancestor} was killed, eleven men were wounded, some severely, and two were missing.[11]

Following Antietam, General Ambrose E. Burnside was placed in command of the Army of the Potomac and, in December, 1862, planned and conducted the campaign ending in the battle of Fredericksburg. On December 10 Battery A, at that time consisting of six three inch rifled cannon, joined the massed artillery of the Left Grand Division of the Army of the Potomac on the heights north of Fredericksburg to protect the engineers bridging the river and the army's left flank during the crossing of the infantry. It participated in the artillery barrage on December 11 and then crossed the river with the division to which it was attached.

The next day the battery was ordered to support the division of General Abner Doubleday of the First Corps and was posted on the extreme left at the river. Here it fired on a Confederate battery, disabled one of its guns and forced it to withdraw. In the afternoon the battery moved to a new position and joined with other batteries against a large concentration of Confederate artillery. One of Wolcott's guns was dismounted shortly after taking this position, killing two men and wounding three others. This gun was from Lieutenant Thomas Binyan's section. At about 2 P.M. the five remaining guns were brought up to the Bowling Green Road to support the assaults by the divisions of generals George G. Meade and John Gibbon.

The battery was relieved on December 14 and returned to its own division. Colonel Charles Wainwright, First Corps Chief of Artillery, stated in his report: "To Captain Wolcott and his battery I am indebted for much very valuable service during the time he was temporarily serving with this corps." General Doubleday wrote of him: "His guns were posted on my right and at once opened on the enemy with excellent effect."[12]

Lieutenant Rigby, in beginning his Fredericksburg letter, tells his father how he came to write it.

> "You will without doubt, be a little surprised at my writing a letter upon such a sheet of paper as this…a battery [had] opened upon us from our extreme left, delivering an ineffective enfilading fire. While we were watching the shells from this gun, whizzing across our rear, someone remarked, if he had a sheet of paper, he would write a letter, when bang went one of those shells, and up flew a quire of paper.
>
> The 14th Brooklyn Regt was lying in our rear; the shell struck the knapsack of one of the men, and knocked it all to pieces, scattering everything in every direction, and among the rest, this paper. So we concluded we would write."

One corner of the letter is badly rumpled from its ordeal.[13]

After the disaster at Fredericksburg, General Burnside attempted an unsuccessful flanking movement, referred to as the "Mud March," and was replaced by General Joseph Hooker. Hooker, in turn, undertook a flanking movement to the northwest of Fredericksburg, which ended in the battle of Chancellorsville. As part of this campaign, General John Sedgwick's Sixth Corps remained at Fredericksburg and engaged Confederate forces left there in what became known as the second battle of Fredericksburg, May 3-4, 1863. Captain Wolcott resigned in December, 1862, and Lieutenant Rigby was promoted to captain and command of the battery that was then referred to as Rigby's. The account of the battery's action in the second battle of Fredericksburg, which was considerable, is largely from Captain Rigby's report.[14]

From April 28 to May 2, Battery A was posted on the heights north of Fredericksburg in the same general area where it was located during the battle of Fredericksburg in the previous December. It crossed the river on the morning of May 3, and took position on the Old Richmond Road directly in

front of two earthworks containing enemy artillery. It engaged these batteries
for several hours until the Federal infantry took the heights south of the city.
During the exchange the battery fired 450 projectiles and one man was
wounded.[15]

Elements of General William T. H. Brooks' Division, including Battery A,
moved over the heights in the early afternoon and up Plank Road toward
Chancellorsville. Opposed by a Confederate brigade, an engagement took
place near the tollgates on Plank Road. In the artillery exchange Sergeant John
Wormsley was severely wounded and died several days later. Near sundown
the Confederates, reinforced from Chancellorsville, attacked in force at Salem
Church. The artillery finally stopped the attack. Battery A used shrapnel and
canister in the right section, but could not employ canister in the left section
because a large number of Federal infantrymen were in front of them.
Nightfall ended this action.[16]

On the morning of May 4, the battery reported to General Albion P.
Howe's Division of the Sixth Corps. It was posted on the Banks Ford Road,
200 yards to the left of the Plank Road, and remained there until about 4 P.M.
when the Confederates launched a heavy attack on Howe's infantry. Battery A
replied with shell and shrapnel. Colonel Charles H. Tompkins, Sixth Corps
Artillery Chief, wrote in his report: "In the evening a most determined attack
was made upon Howe's front...Martin and Ribgy both did excellent execution,
fighting desperately, but with coolness and judgment, and only falling back to
a second position when their supports had left them...In his attack upon this
line, the enemy was repulsed with great slaughter, the batteries rendering very
efficient service." He specifically recommended Captain Rigby, among others,
for promotion.[17]

Captain Rigby reported that the Twentieth New York retreated through
the battery and when the foe was about 80 yards away he gave the order to
withdraw. The movement was made difficult because of the retreating New
Yorkers. The horses of one limber stampeded, leaving the gun behind. Captain
Rigby, at sabre point, forced some of the infantrymen to pull off the gun by
hand and soon reunited it with its limber. The Third Vermont then counter
charged and drove the enemy back. Another of Rigby's men was wounded in
this action.

For the remaining daylight hours the battery was posted on the left of

Howe's line. It was then ordered back to its own division and re-crossed the river on the night of the 4th. During the day it fired 985 projectiles. General Howe said in his report that Rigby's and another battery "...were largely instrumental in breaking the attack of the enemy's left."[18]

After the Chancellorsville campaign, General George G. Meade replaced General Hooker as commander of the Army of the Potomac and commanded the army at the battle of Gettysburg. Rigby's battery was detached from the Sixth Corps and assigned to the Artillery Reserve.[19]

On the morning of July 2, 1863, Battery A was posted on Powers Hill, one mile south of the town of Gettysburg and 500 yards west of the Baltimore Turnpike in support of Major General Henry W. Slocum's Twelfth Corps which constituted the Federal right flank. Here it fired on an enemy battery 2,500 yards away for a short time. On the afternoon of July 2, part of the Twelfth Corps was withdrawn to support the Federal left and the Confederates captured the first line of earthworks on Culp's Hill in a night attack.[20]

At dawn on July 3 Rigby's battery and others were ordered by General Slocum to open fire on the enemy troops in this area in order to drive them off the hill. Captain Rigby kept up a slow fire for about three hours and said that General Slocum told him "...that the battery did terrible execution." The battery remained on Powers Hill until Sunday afternoon, July 5, when it was ordered to report back to Artillery Reserve. A monument to Battery A stands on Powers Hill near its position during the battle and Captain Rigby gave the dedication address.[21]

Returns after Gettysburg show Lieutenant Thomas Binyon in command of the battery, Captain Rigby being on medical leave at this time. In November of 1863 the battery was transferred from the Artillery Reserve to the artillery of the First Corps under Colonel Charles S. Wainwright.[22]

The opposing armies then maneuvered in Northern Virginia in the Bristoe Campaign, October 9 through November 9, and the Mine Run Campaign, November 26 through December 1, 1863. During this period, Battery A was part of the artillery brigade of the First Corps. The Corps was not engaged in the battle of Bristoe Station, the only engagement of these two campaigns. The battery did participate in a demonstration on the Rapidan River by the First Corps, February 6 and 7, 1864. This was its last active service with the Army of the Potomac.[23]

Artist's rendering of Wolcott's Battery, First Maryland Light Artillery engaged at the Battle of Antietam on September 17, 1862. (D.C.T.)

In April of 1864 the battery was assigned to duty in the defenses of Washington, first in the light artillery camp of instruction and later in one of the forts surrounding the city. In June the battery was ordered to be remounted but in July, during the third Confederate invasion of the North, it was sent to Harper's Ferry, West Virginia, as infantry. It remained in the Department of West Virginia as infantry for the remainder of its service.[24]

In September and October 1864 the three-year terms of service of the original enlistees expired. Some men reenlisted as veteran volunteers and the ranks were augmented by new recruits. The battery was consolidated with Battery B, First Maryland Light Artillery in March, 1865, one month before the Army of Northern Virginia surrendered at Appomattox Court House.[25]

Battery A's first captain, John W. Wolcott, was an accountant and broker in civilian life. He was the only battery commander who was not a Marylander by birth or choice. A resident of Roxbury, Massachusetts, when the war began, he enlisted as a First Lieutenant in the Second Massachusetts Light Artillery. Why he was chosen as captain of Battery A, First Maryland Light Artillery is not clear. Lieutenant Rigby, who was Senior First Lieutenant and had prior artillery experience, would seem to have been the logical choice.

In a letter written after the Battle of Antietam to the wounded Lieutenant John Bigelow, adjutant of Maryland's Gist Artillery Battalion, Mrs. Wolcott wrote of her husband: "He was often posted in the most exposed positions and we hear by letters from the First Massachusetts Battery that the Captain was covered all over with glory. In his quiet way when writing he says of himself 'I have shown that I aint afierd(sic) and have been reported to General F [General Franklin, his Corps Commander] for execution of my battery and personal bravery.'"[26]

Captain James H. Rigby was born in Baltimore, June 4, 1831. A carpenter by trade, he was, at the beginning of the war, a member of the Eagle Battery, a Baltimore militia unit. He was mustered in as First Lieutenant of Battery A in August 1861 and was promoted to captain and assumed command of the battery in December 1862. Rigby was present for the entire period of service of the battery except for a short period in the latter part of 1863, when he was on medical leave for treatment of an eye condition.

Captain Rigby was an articulate man and wrote well. The three existing letters he wrote to his family from the field graphically describe his experiences and feelings during the war. He was an ardent Union man as is evident from these words contained in his letter from the field at Fredericksburg: "If I should fall in this battle…you may rest assured that it will be with my face to the foe. Teach my children that I fell fighting for the flag that has always protected Virtue, Honor, and Independence, and punished Vice, Oppression and Tyranny."

Captain Rigby survived the war and died in 1889, after a period of declining health. He is buried in the Old National Cemetery in Baltimore and on his grave stone is inscribed "A Valiant Soldier in Defense of the Union," as indeed he was.[27]

During its term of service the battery's total casualties were six enlisted men killed or mortally wounded and twenty-eight enlisted men who died of disease. In addition, there were an unknown number of wounded. Although the battery had one gun disabled by enemy artillery fire, it did not have a single gun captured on the field of battle. In addition to Captain Wolcott's guidon, several of its other battle flags are preserved at the Maryland State Archives in Annapolis, the state capital.[28]

BATTERY B
FIRST MARYLAND
LIGHT ARTILLERY
UNITED STATES
VOLUNTEERS

Battery B, First Maryland Light Artillery, United States Volunteers, was organized in Baltimore and Pikesville, Maryland, and was mustered into service in September and October, 1862, as part of the Purnell Legion. Most of the members were from Port Deposit and its vicinity in Cecil County, Maryland. Jacob Tome, founder of the fashionable school of the time in Cecil County, was said to be instrumental in the recruitment of the battery and to have supported it financially. Alonzo Snow served as its captain throughout the war, and it is generally known as Snow's Battery.[1]

The battery began its service under General John A. Dix's command in Baltimore and was soon assigned to duty on the eastern shore of Maryland. It participated in the campaign against Confederate forces in the two Virginia counties south of the Maryland state line on the Delmarva Peninsula as described in the history of the Gist Artillery Battalion.

In June 1862 Battery B joined the Army of the Potomac during the Peninsula Campaign. The battery, consisting of six three inch rifled cannon, was assigned to the artillery reserve of the army then engaged with Confederate troops south west of Richmond. After the battle of Seven Pines the Army of the Potomac was in retreat to a new base at Harrison's Landing.[2]

Battery B, supporting the Fifth Corps, was posted at one of the bridges spanning the Chickahominy River which the corps had to cross during the retreat. On June 5, 1862, just three days after joining the army, the battery saw its first action. General Henry J. Hunt, commander of the Artillery Reserve, noted in his report that "…the enemy opened a heavy fire from several distinct points on our positions, principally upon that near the New Bridge occupied by Snow's Battery. The fire was returned with spirit by that battery which [aided by others] soon silenced their fire and drove them off."[3]

Positioned in a cornfield near the bridge, the battery opened fire on Confederate infantry visible across the river and drove them back into the woods. About 8 A.M. the Confederates opened with four batteries. According to Snow's report, Battery B "…returned their fire, dividing it among the four batteries according to the excellence of their range, and silenced each in succession from their right to left…," expending 630 rounds of shell and case shot in the process. The battery's position was extremely muddy and the caissons and limbers sank to their axles, requiring that the teams be unhitched and the pieces be hauled by hand.[4]

General Fitz-John Porter, commanding the Fifth Corps, wrote on July 9, 1862, "I was present at the skirmish of the First Maryland Battery with the enemy, and have to commend the admirable manner in which it was maneuvered and served, subjected as it was to a hot fire from various directions, and from some guns at pretty close range. I was struck with the coolness of the men and officers, who I believed were for the first time under fire."[5]

The Federal retreat continued on down the peninsula to the new base at Harrison's Landing where the final battle of the campaign was fought. This was the battle of Malvern Hill, July 1, 1862, which involved one of the heaviest concentrations of artillery during the entire war.[6]

The two Maryland batteries, A and B, were initially posted on the right of the Federal Line on a plateau atop the hill. Battery B was then sent to reinforce Couch's Division on the left. Positioned in a field, it dueled with a Confederate battery which stood in a field of oats covered by stacked and standing grain. Snow's Battery destroyed one piece with its men and teams and drove the battery off. It was replaced by a second which was also forced to retire by the accuracy of Battery B's fire.

This action took about an hour during which two men were severely wounded by sharpshooters who were very active. The battery was then disbursed. First the left section under Lieutenant Vanneman, then the center section under Lieutenant Kidd were posted elsewhere, leaving the right section under Lieutenant Gerry still in its original position and still the target of the sharpshooters who wounded four more men.

Vanneman, now in the center of the line, and Kidd on the left, were exposed to heavy infantry fire and the battery was not reassembled until the close of the battle. It left the field between 9 and 10 o'clock that night. Lieutenant Vanneman was severely wounded by shell fragments in the chest and both legs. Adjutant Bigelow of the Artillery Brigade, who replaced him, was also wounded. Total casualties amounted to two killed and eighteen wounded, some of whom had to be left on the field.[7]

During the first Confederate invasion of the North, the Army of the Potomac moved north to protect Washington and the two armies clashed at South Mountain near Frederick, Maryland. Snow's Battery was now attached to the Second Division (Smith's) of the Sixth Corps (Franklin's). The Sixth Corps fought the battle of Crampton's Gap on September 14, 1862. This was the most southern of the three passes comprising the South Mountain battlefield. While present on the field, the battery was not actively engaged.[8]

The Sixth Corps arrived at Antietam in the late morning of September 17 and was posted on the right flank of the army after most of the action in that sector was over. Captain Snow was ill and Lieutenant Vanneman, recovered from his Malvern Hill wounds, was in command. The battery took position in a cornfield near Division Headquarters and shelled the woods in their front, known forever after as the West Woods. A Confederate battery, which was probably the Confederate Baltimore Battery (there was also a Federal Baltimore battery) returned the fire and was eventually silenced. The battery experienced no casualties at Antietam except for one horse that was hit by a six pound shot. The battery expended 300 rounds of ammunition.[9]

Battery B – Snow's: Officers of Battery B, Maryland Light Artillery. 1st Lt James H. Kidd, 2nd Lt Lenard S. Parker, 1st Lt Lucius A. Gerry, 1st Lt T. J. Vannerman, Captain Alonzo Snow. (D.C.T.)

In the early morning hours of the day following the battle, while still in place on the field, Lieutenant Vannerman wrote a letter to his wife in which he expressed his horror at what he had been through. This, in part, is what he said:

> "Thank God that none of out battery were killed in the terrible battle of yesterday…The rebels have suffered heavily. In one place not fifty yards from our right piece… in a space not longer that (the) above are 33 dead rebels…and all around their dead bodies lie. You can not move in any way but what you will see them…their mangled forms look horrible. In one body there were seventeen bullets and others shot in all shapes and forms imaginable. Such a sight I never want to see again and I never want to spend another night on a battlefield.
>
> The cries of the wounded and dying can not help but melt the hardest heart. One poor rebel who I had given water to a number of times in the afternoon called out to me in the middle of the night to please to please give him water. Some of the men supplied his wants. How he fares now I do not know as he was moved this morning…The cannonading was a great deal heavier than at Malvern Hills, and I thought that was perfectly awful, but this throws it entirely in the shade."[10]

After Antietam, General McClellan was replaced as commander of the Army of the Potomac by General Ambrose E. Burnside who ultimately faced the Army of Northern Virginia at Fredericksburg, in the next great battle in the eastern theater.

On December 12, 1862, the Sixth Corps crossed the Rappahannock River downstream from Fredericksburg as part of the Left Grand Division. Snow's Battery was posted to the left of the Second (Howe's) Division at a place called Deep Run. Two Confederate batteries were directly in front of Snow and about 800 yards away.

The Battle of Fredericksburg was fought the next day. It began with a heavy exchange of artillery fire, opened in the morning by Snow's Battery. After one hour the Confederate battery withdrew. A second exchange took place in the afternoon for about an hour, which dismounted one Confederate gun and destroyed several caissons. Sporadic firing continued during the rest of day and for a third time the Confederate gunners were driven off. Although there was little firing on the fourteenth, the battery was continuously harassed by Confederate sharpshooters. The guns were withdrawn to the north bank of the river on December 15. Captain Romeyn Ayres, Sixth Corps Chief of Artillery, noted in his report that "Herekimer's and Snow's batteries did some good shooting."[11]

After the disaster at Fredericksburg, Burnside was replaced by Major General Joseph Hooker who attempted a massive flanking movement around the Confederate left which culminated in the Battle of Chancellorsville, May 2-3, 1863. In General Order Number 18, Issued March 3, 1863, Hooker states among other things, "...the inspection reports of the following regiments and batteries giving evidence of the necessity of strong exertions on the part of every officer and member of the command to bring them into a proper state of discipline and efficiency, no further leaves of absence or furloughs will be granted to these commands and all officers absent therefrom must be recalled and their leaves revoked." Listed among the batteries was Snow's which, at that time, was still probably attached to the Sixth Corps.[12]

On March 30 the battery was assigned to the brigade of Brigadier General Marsena Patrick, the Provost Marshall General of the army, in the defense of Aquia Creek Landing and the railroad to Falmouth, the main supply line to the army at Fredericksburg. The organization of the Army of the Potomac for May 1-6, 1863, the period covering the Chancellorsville campaign, shows Snow's Battery still attached to Patrick's Brigade (Colonel William F. Rogers commanding), reporting directly to General Headquarters of the army. It remained in and around Aquia Creek Landing and did not take an active part in the battle of Chancellorsville. By May 31 Patrick's Brigade was disbanded and Battery B was assigned to the Artillery Reserve.[13]

On June 25, 1863, the battery was ordered to report to the artillery camp of instruction at Arlington Heights, Virginia. Meanwhile, the Confederate army was beginning its movement north, which would culminate in the battle of Gettysburg. The battery remained at Arlington Heights for only a short period of time before it was moved into the defenses of Washington and then transferred to Baltimore City. There on July 2 Captain Snow was appointed

Chief of Artillery of the defenses of that city. After the Battle of Gettysburg the battery was reassigned to the Army of the Potomac which it joined at Frederick, Maryland, on July 6.[14]

However, the order was changed and Snow's Battery was assigned to the Department of West Virginia and went instead to Maryland Heights opposite Harper's Ferry. It remained in and around Harper's Ferry in a number of different commands for about nine months during part of which time Captain Snow served as Chief of Artillery for the command. On April 17, 1864, the battery left for Martinsburg, West Virginia, to take part in Major General Franz Sigel's movement up Shenandoah Valley. Battery B was now part of the artillery of General Sullivan's Division of which Captain Snow was Chief of Artillery.[15]

Sigel's advance terminated in the battle of New Market, Virginia, in which the boys of the cadet corps of the Virginia Military Institute took part. On May 14, Colonel Augustus Moor, leading the advance with two sections of Battery B in his command, occupied a position just north of New Market and the artillery opened fire to develop the position of the Confederates whose own artillery soon replied. A heavy column of infantry then advanced on Moor's position, but the fire of Lieutenant Gerry's section of Battery B stopped them. Moor's line fell back some 800 yards to the top of a hill with the Eighteenth Connecticut Infantry acting as support for the battery. The Marylander's nearly changed the course of history when a three inch shell from one of Snow's guns struck a post in the courtyard of Saint Matthew's Lutheran Church while General Breckenridge sat on his horse only five yards away observing the battle through his field glasses. The shell embedded itself in the wooden post, but failed to explode.[16]

When the final battle lines were formed just north of New Market, Snow's Battery was posted on the extreme right of the Federal line, against the north fork of the Shenandoah River, and opened fire just as the Confederate advance began. The colonel of the Eighteenth Connecticut wrote, "…the cannonading was at this time extremely rapid, the rebels shelling our position with great accuracy, while the batteries of our first and second lines poured grape and canister into their infantry, which came on in splendid line." Smoke from infantry fire and the batteries on the right became so thick that it was impossible to tell friend from foe.

Camp chair: Folding camp chair used by Lt. Gerry During the war. Manufacturer's label on back reads, "No 4 Premium camp chair Patented Aug 20, 1860 Oct 6, 1863 Re-issued July 5 and Aug 13, 1865." (D.C.T.)

When the Federal left finally gave way under the Confederate attack, Sigel gave orders for the artillery to withdraw by sections from the right flank to new positions on Rude's Hill to the rear of the main line. Captain Snow wrote that, "… on this hill the battery made its last stand on the day of the fight and retired slowly and sullenly feeling they were made to retire without cause." As the army fell back across the Shenandoah River, Battery B, under the command of Lieutenant Gerry, protected the rear guard.[17]

Shortly after the battle of New Market, Captain Snow, with several of his officers, toured the battlefield and recorded this poignant description in his diary.

"Little remains to show of the furious strife only two weeks ago—a few new made [graves] and dead horses are [all] that is to [be] seen worthy of note—In a lime kiln the rebels had thrown about thirty of our dead mostly with their faces down and had a slight covering of earth over them but not enough to hide them from view...

Qtr Master Bacon of the 14 Mass regiment found his brother who [was] killed and left on the field he has had [a] box made and put the body in interred in a secure place [where] he can be found as he intends ordering a metallic coffin and have his body sent home.

Many of our wounded are in New Market and speak in high terms of the kindness of some of the people—a number I found in a barn on the battle ground—they say the citizens treated them kindly..."[18]

After the Federal defeat at New Market, Sigel was replaced by General David Hunter who led the Federal forces in the ill-fated Lynchburg campaign in which Snow's Battery participated. Under Hunter the artillery was brigaded and Captain Snow resumed command of the battery.

The Federal objective was the capture of the city of Lynchburg, an important transportation and supply center. The campaign began well enough in the Battle of Piedmont on June 5, 1864. With the Confederates well posted, the battle was begun at 9 A.M. by the artillery. General Hunter noted in his reported that "At 11:30 the fine practice of our artillery had silenced the enemy's batteries." In this sharp artillery exchange Snow's Battery moved up to within 450 yards of and silenced a Confederate battery which had been damaging the infantry. Several infantry attacks and counter attacks followed throughout the afternoon. The Federal forces finally hit successfully the center and both flanks and drove the Confederates from the field. General William E. Jones, the Confederate commander, was killed and about 1,000 prisoners were taken.[19]

Hunter's army then advanced, via Stauton and Lexington, and approached Lynchburg on the Bedford Turnpike. He was delayed for several hours at the Great Otter River because of the difficulty in getting the artillery across. By the morning of June 13, 1864, the infantry divisions were before the Confederate works outside Lynchburg, the artillery being posted in commanding positions on either flank. The Confederates attacked about 2 P.M. and were repulsed and forced back into their fortifications. According to General Hunter, "The artillery, which materially assisted in repelling the attack, was served with remarkable rapidity and efficiency." Snow's Battery, on the left of the Federal line in a plowed field, was once again supported by the Eighteenth Connecticut, the same regiment which had been their support at New Market. As the Confederate fire grew more intense on Snow, the First Kentucky Artillery moved to the extreme left of the line to draw the fire away from the battery.

At this point, Hunter, being low on ammunition and believing himself heavily outnumbered, retreated, not the way he had come, but to the north west through the rugged West Virginia mountains. Lieutenant Gerry's section supported the cavalry that acted as a rear guard.[20]

On June 21, 1864, near a place called Salem, disaster struck Snow's Battery. The artillery had been sent off during a rear guard action without infantry support. While they were watering the horses in Mason Cove Creek, a brigade of Confederate cavalry attacked and the Federals lost eight guns with limbers and four caissons. Snow's loss was four guns. Many prisoners were taken, including Captain Von Kleiser of the Thirtieth New York Battery. Lieutenant Kidd and twenty-five others of Snow's men were among those captured, and a number of them died while prisoners of war. Known to have perished at Andersonville were privates John C. Brown, Thomas P. Reed and Andrew J. Van Court. Privates John Simmes and Phillip Williams died in the lesser-known prison at Florence, South Carolina.[21]

Hunter's army continued its difficult retreat through the mountains and eventually reached Charleston, about July 1, 1864. Snow's battery continued to serve in the Department of West Virginia and, for a time, was part of a brigade under the command of Brigadier General Rutherford B. Hayes, a future president of the United States.[22]

The battery was posted to Cumberland, Maryland, on July 25, 1864, and took position at Fort Number 1 on a hill overlooking the city. Four days later word was received that enemy troops were advancing on Cumberland via the National Pike from Hancock, Maryland. This was the cavalry command of

Brigadier General John McCausland returning from Chambersburg, Pennsylvania, having burned that city in retaliation for similar actions by Hunter in the Shenandoah Valley. Snow's Battery and other troops of the Cumberland command met them in the afternoon about three miles from town. Heavy firing was kept up until dark and the Confederates withdrew that night.[23]

At the time of the state and national elections in November 1864, eighty men of Battery B were given leave to return home to vote. In the polling which took place at the battery, the vote was 17 for President Lincoln, 0 for General McClellan.[24]

Although the battery remained in the Department of West Virginia until the end of the war, the defense of Cumberland was the last time it saw combat. It was mustered out of service on July 3, 1865, almost four years after its formation.[25]

A native of Vermont, Captain Alonzo Snow was a prominent merchant in Port Deposit, Cecil County, Maryland, when he enlisted in August 1861. He was 55, rather old for active field service; however, he had served a five-year enlistment in the regular army as a member of the Fourth United States Artillery, which is probably why he was chosen to be captain of the battery. While stationed at Fort McHenry in Baltimore he met the girl who became his wife.

Except for several periods of absence due to illness, and three assignments as Chief of Artillery for various commands, he commanded the battery which bore his name from August 1861 to July 1865. After the war Captain Snow was postmaster at Port Deposit for many years until forced to resign because of ill health. He died in Baltimore at the age of 77 and is buried in Louden Park Cemetery in that city.[26]

The surviving members of Snow's Battery began holding reunions in 1887. As in many small towns across America, these were elaborate, all day affairs for which the entire town turned out. The *Cecil Whig* reported of the 1890 reunion:

> "On last Saturday Port Deposit was decorated with bunting in honor of the reunion of Battery B, First Maryland Light Artillery known as Snow's Battery. Nearly every dwelling and

store had our national insignia floating in the breeze. The reunion was held in the town hall...At 1:30 P.M. the soldiers formed in procession with River Side Band in the lead, followed by a number of wounded comrades in carriages, and marched through the town."

In 1894 the reunion took place in the G.A.R. Hall in North East, Maryland, and a feature of the usual parade was a flag with a star shot out by Confederate gunners at Lynchburg thirty years before. The ladies of the Perryville Methodist Church served a fine dinner for 25 cents when the church hosted the reunion.

The last reunion of Battery B, Maryland Light Artillery was held in 1926, sixty one years after the war with no plans to meet again due to diminishing membership. When Private Henry Jackson died in 1939, at the age of 93, he was probably the last survivor of Snow's Battery.[27]

BALTIMORE BATTERY MARYLAND LIGHT ARTILLERY UNITED STATES VOLUNTEERS

A third battery of Maryland Light Artillery was organized for the United States Volunteer Service at Baltimore in August of 1862 for a term of three years or the duration of the war. It logically would have been designated as Battery C but instead was named the Baltimore Battery and was also known as Alexander's Battery after its captain, Frederic W. Alexander. There was also a Confederate Baltimore Battery in the Army of Northern Virginia. The two would meet on the field of battle.[1]

The battery trained in Baltimore, during which time two of its guns were posted at Relay to guard the railroad and the Thomas Viaduct. It was then assigned to the defenses of the Upper Potomac and reported to General John

R. Kenly at Williamsport where it became part of the Maryland Brigade and remained until December. While there an experimental gun, invented by Captain Alexander, exploded during a test, killing a drummer boy in the Eighth Maryland Infantry and wounding several other soldiers. The battery was transferred to Maryland Heights, across the river from Harper's Ferry, where it remained on duty until the following Spring.[2]

In April of 1863 the Battery was temporarily assigned to the Division of Major General Robert H. Milroy which held an advanced position in the Shenandoah Valley near Winchester, Virginia. On April 27 it arrived at Berryville, a few miles north of Winchester, where it relieved a West Virginia battery.[3]

After the battle of Chancellorsville in May of 1863 Confederate authorities decided to launch the second invasion of the North. The Army of Northern Virginia began to advance down the Shenandoah Valley in route to Pennsylvania. On the morning of June 13 General Richards S. Ewell appeared at Berryville.[4]

The brigade of Colonel A. T. McReynolds, to which the battery was attached, was ordered to join the main force at Winchester. The brigade withdrew under attack with two sections of the battery accompanying the infantry and the third section under Captain Alexander, with the First New York Cavalry, forming the rear guard. The cavalry commander reported "...the vigorous support of Lieutenant Alexander who served these two guns most gallantly and with terrible effect upon the advancing columns of the enemy." The Confederate van again attacked the Federal rear guard at the crossing of Opequon Creek and a counter charge by the cavalry was supported by Captain Alexander and part of the Sixth Maryland Infantry. Alexander had crossed the creek but returned with one gun and opened with canister, which stopped the Confederate advance.[5]

McReynolds' brigade arrived at Winchester late in the evening of Saturday, June 13, after having fought twice during the day at Berryville and Opequon Creek. It took a position in a fortification known as the Star Fort north of the city and near the Main Fort where General Milroy had his headquarters. On Sunday morning one section of the battery was ordered to a hill north of the fort. About noon Lieutenant Leary's section was assigned to operate with General Washington L. Elliott's brigade outside and north of the Star

Fort. Here skirmishing occurred most of the day with the Baltimore Battery exchanging fire at one time with its Confederate counterpart. One of Alexander's men had a brother serving in the rebel battery. Taking a position behind the infantry, Leary fired over the heads of the Federal skirmishers into the woods where the Confederates were concealed. The other two sections remained in the Star Fort.[6]

At about 6 o'clock in the evening the Confederates attacked a detachment of infantry and artillery holding a partially completed earthwork about 2,000 yards from the Main Fort. They captured Battery L, Fifth U.S. Artillery and forced the infantry and the Fifth West Virginia Artillery to seek the shelter of the Main Fort. Alexander's two sections withdrew into the Star Fort. The sections already in the fort helped to cover the retreat. Three Confederate batteries then shelled both forts, eventually concentrating their fire on the Marylanders. Returning fire at a range of 1,500 to 1,700 yards, the Baltimore Battery forced them to change position three times, destroying two guns, a limber and a caisson in the process. Captain Alexander and his officers frequently sighted the guns themselves and the exchange lasted until dark. So heavy had been the firing throughout the day that the battery's ammunition was reduced from 1,200 rounds to 168 rounds (from 200 rounds to 28 rounds per gun).

A major attack appearing imminent, the Sixth Maryland Infantry was placed inside the Star Fort and the Seventy-sixth Pennsylvania Infantry in the surrounding rifle pits. Alexander's guns loaded with canister and awaited an attack that never came.[7]

Milroy's Division of about 9,000 men was now completely surrounded by a Confederate Corps and on the night of June 1 the general held a council of war with his brigade commanders. It was decided to abandon the forts and attempt to escape under cover of the darkness to the North and safety. To accomplish this without the Confederates' knowledge would require complete silence so the noise of wheels could not be tolerated. Therefore the artillery and all other rolling stock had to be abandoned and destroyed. When Captain Alexander received orders to spike his guns and destroy the battery's equipment and supplies he protested and asked permission to take his battery out on the retreat but his request was denied. Consequently he "...spiked the guns, disabled the carriages, destroyed the ammunition and removed and destroyed

Private Frederick Miller: Entered the service on February 27, 1864, and was discharged with the battery on June 17, 1865. (Wild)

the traces and the trace-chains, which would rattle." His men left two by two on the battery horses, and on foot, bringing up the rear with the cavalry regiment. The Federal column was intercepted about five-mile north of Winchester near Stevenson's Depot on the Winchester and Potomac Railroad and a sharp fight ensued in which it was overwhelmed and many captured.[8]

The unarmed artillerymen were completely defenseless against the Confederate attack. Captain Alexander ordered them to try and escape through the woods on either side of the turnpike. He would rather have taken them out in a body but their formation had been disorganized due to the intrusion of a large number of teamsters among them. One group under Captain Alexander made its way back to Harper's Ferry. Another, under his brother, Lieutenant Eugene Alexander, crossed the Potomac River into Maryland at Sr. John's Run. The Baltimore Battery's casualties were one killed, three wounded and about fifty missing, most of whom were taken prisoner.[9]

Frederick W. Wild, one of those captured, wrote of his experiences as a prisoner of war. After the confusion of the battery's dispersal he found himself alone, surrounded by Confederates, one of whom relieved him of his horse and cap. He recognized a passing cavalryman as a former schoolmate who stopped to talk to him briefly. In spite of his unenviable position, Wild still found a touch of humor in the sight of a Confederate soldier passing by, laden down with captured regimental band instruments, and "…tooting a large horn for all he was worth."

The prisoners were eventually rounded up and taken in charge by a Maryland unit [probably the Second Maryland Infantry] some of whom proved to be friends and neighbors. They were well treated and collaborated with their captors in stealing food out of General Milroy's commissary tent which was then under Confederate guard. The spoils were shared among the Marylanders, Rebels and Yankees alike.

One of the most difficult times for the prisoners of war was the train ride to Richmond. They were packed tight into freight cars, some of which still bore traces of their former equine occupants. After a brief stop at the famous Libby Prison, Alexander's men were transferred to Belle Isle, the enlisted men's prison camp on the James River. They had only been there a few days when twelve more members of the Baltimore Battery arrived. Eleven of these unfortunate fellows had made it back safely to Harper's Ferry and had decided to go home to Baltimore without leave. The twelfth had not even been in the battle but was returning from furlough and had decided to join them. They were hardly under way when their train was captured at Point of Rocks by Confederate cavalry and they ended up in Richmond instead.

Alexander's men were fortunate indeed, for their incarceration lasted less than a month. Belle Isle was not overly crowded at this time and they at least got a bare minimum to eat. Thirty-six members of the battery were released several days after the fourth of July and were sent by train to City Point, Virginia. When the boys riding on top of the cars saw the Stars and Stripes flying on the exchange boat, they broke out into wild cheering, dancing and jumping up and down, almost causing the roofs to collapse. The former prisoners arrived at Camp Parole in Annapolis, Maryland, on July 9, 1863, and shortly thereafter rejoined the battery in Baltimore.[10]

There was a lengthy court of inquiry to investigate the circumstances and responsibilities of Milroy's defeat which exonerated him from blame. Captain Alexander was one of the witnesses called before the court and testified at length. He described in detail the actions of his battery during the three days and, when asked if he thought he could have saved his guns, said he did not know but would liked to have tried.[11]

Captain Alexander's men were reunited at Baltimore where the battery was remounted and equipped with six three inch rifled cannon and was then stationed on North Avenue between Greenmount Avenue and St. Paul Street at the site of the present Polytechnic Institute. It remained on duty in the defenses of Baltimore for almost a year. It was sent to Harper's Ferry in February of 1864 to oppose a threatened attack on that place, which never materialized, and then returned to Baltimore as part of the northwest defenses of the city. During a part of this time Captain Alexander was Chief of Artillery and was also detailed to special recruiting duty by order of the Adjutant General's office. The battery would again see action during the third Confederate invasion of the North in July 1864.[12]

On July 5, 1864, Captain Alexander was ordered to bring the battery to Monocacy Junction near Frederick City. Federal authorities now knew that a large force believed to be that of Major General Jubal A. Early's Second Corps of the Army of Northern Virginia had crossed the Potomac River some where northwest of Frederick. General Lew Wallace, who was commanding the Middle Department with headquarters at Baltimore, hastened to gather together the few troops available in his department to feel out and contest this advance. The logical place to do so was at Monocacy Junction, a few miles south of Frederick where the roads from Washington and Baltimore converged. Here the Confederate objective, be it Baltimore or the Capitol, would be disclosed and, hopefully, Wallace could delay them long enough for defensive measures to be taken to protect the target city. The division of General James B. Ricketts of the Sixth Corps, Army of the Potomac, had been sent north from the Richmond-Petersburg front to join Wallace and most of it arrived in time to participate in the Battle of Monocacy.[13]

On the morning of July 7, Wallace sent the Eighth Illinois Cavalry, with two guns of the Baltimore Battery under Lieutenant Peter Leary, west on the National Pike from Frederick to develop the position and strength of the Confederates reported to be in the vicinity of Boonsboro. They met the Confederate advance a few miles outside of Frederick near Middletown. Outnumbered, the Eighth Illinois and Leary skirmished with the Confederates and gradually fell back to Catacton Mountain from where Leary's guns, being advantageously placed, slowed the Confederate skirmishers. But the small Federal force was soon outflanked and withdrew from the mountain.[14]

On the outskirts of Frederick it was reinforced by a third gun of the battery, under the direct command of Captain Alexander, and the Third

the morning, "...all was so calm and white, and the numerous mounds looked like so many graves, all was as quiet as a city of the dead, and when the bugle blew, and the dark forms arose out of the snow, one of the boys remarked, that it looked like Resurrection Day." The battery remained at Camp Berry for the rest of the war. At 2:30 A.M. on April 10, 1865, it fired a salute in honor of the Confederate surrender at Appomattox Court House the day before. After the assassination of President Lincoln the mounted members of the battery formed part of a vast picket line around the city in an attempt to apprehend John Wilkes Booth. He passed over the road where they were assigned about an hour before they arrived.[26]

The battery continued on duty at Camp Barry until June 8, 1865, when it was mustered out of the Volunteer Service of the United States. The men proceeded to Baltimore and received their discharge papers at Camp Bradford (now Lafayette Square) on June 17, 1865.[27]

Captain Alexander, a member of a prominent Baltimore family, was the eldest son of John Henry Alexander, a widely known scientist, author, engineer and topographer. John Henry Alexander, at the beginning of the war, was Engineering Officer on the staff of the Middle Department Commander and laid out the defenses of Baltimore.[28]

Frederic W. Alexander was a Civil Engineer and inventor. His inventions, among other weaponry innovations, included new style bayonets, prototypes of which survive at the Maryland Historical Society. He also wrote a manual on how to make battery maneuvers to bulge calls. He had been appointed First Assistant Examiner in the United States Patent Office in July 1862 but could not take the position because of his impending enlistment.[29]

During his term of service Captain Alexander was several times sought for assignment to special duty. In February 1863 General Robert Schenck, commanding the Eighth Army Corps with headquarters at Baltimore, requested his services "...to help me by some advice in details and also in a degree by his considerable personal influence in the enlistment of [a] new battery." In 1864 he was again sought to recruit and train a new heavy artillery regiment and served during the latter part of the war at Eighth Corps headquarters as a member of a military commission.[30]

In his autobiography, General Lew Wallace, commander of the Union forces at the battle of Monocacy, describes his meeting with the captain as follows:

"In Captain Alexander of the battery I found a gentleman looking like a college professor. He accompanied me while riding through his bivouac. I left him with the feeling that a man of his evident good breeding could not be ignorant of the service to which he had attached himself or of the fearless kind in battle. If the worse came, the possibilities were I should consider myself fortunate in having him."[31]

Due to the wound he suffered at Monocacy, Captain Alexander resigned his command of the Baltimore Battery on April 7, 1865, to accept an appointment as Commissary of Subsistence. He served in this capacity until January 10, 1866, when he was mustered out of the army, having received two brevets as major and lieutenant colonel for outstanding war service. He studied law after the war and in 1866 applied for the position of Assistant Patent Examiner with the endorsement of the governor of Maryland, both United States senators, and several members of Congress. Captain Alexander did not long survive the war. He died in 1876, at the age of 39, and is buried in the family plot in Baltimore's Green Mount Cemetery.[32]

He was succeeded briefly by his brother, H. Eugene Alexander, as captain of the Baltimore Battery, who became a Wall Street banker after the war.[33]

First Lieutenant Peter Leary, Jr., had a distinguished post war career. After serving as personal secretary to Governor of Maryland Thomas Swann, he was appointed Second Lieutenant of Artillery in the regular army by President Johnson. He participated in several western campaigns against the Indians, including the famous Chief Joseph, and retired as a brigadier general after thirty-seven years of service.[34]

The post war careers of others of Alexander's men covered a wide range of occupations and ranged from millionaires to paupers. Among the professions were a physician, a dentist and a lawyer. In the political realm, one became a state senator, another a county clerk and a third a member of the Lighthouse Board. Of the two who joined the regular army, in addition to Lieutenant Leary, one was killed by Indians and the other eventually retired to the soldiers' home in Washington.[35]

BATTERY D MARYLAND LIGHT ARTILLERY UNITED STATES VOLUNTEERS

Battery D First Maryland Light Artillery was mustered into the volunteer service of the United States February 29, 1864, in Baltimore, Maryland for three years. The battery was trained in Baltimore and was assigned to the Third Separate Brigade, commanded by General Henry Lockwood, as part of the Eighth Army Corps and served in the defenses of the city. Its Captain was John M. Bruce, a forty-eight-year-old coppersmith from Baltimore County. Bruce had previously served as Captain of Battery A, Second Maryland Light Artillery, a six month unit know as the Junior Battery.[1]

The routine of garrison duty was broken in May by the Valiant affair. Corporal James B. Valiant, a 21-year-old painter in civilian life, was detailed for special duty at the Provost Marshall's office in Baltimore on May 2, 1864. On May 28 he was ordered, with two privates, to take into custody battery members in Baltimore without passes. With two men already under arrest, the party entered Fritz's Lager Beer Garden on Belair Road, over the objections of the door-keeper, and apprehended a third soldier. Valiant and his detail departed, took a fourth man into custody and returned to the beer garden where he thought he had seen another member of the battery. He left two prisoners with one guard at the gate. The other guard and the remaining prisoners started with him back into the hall but were stopped by Sergeant Richard M. Pryor of the Baltimore City Police Department, under whom he had served in the Junior Battery.

Sergeant Pryor refused him permission to enter the hall, cursed Captain Bruce, his former commander, and told Corporal Valiant that if he tried to draw his saber he would blow his head off. Valiant wisely left it in his scabbard. Pryor, claiming he "…could whip any d….d man in the battery…," then took Corporal Valiant into custody and marched him off to the police station where he was forcibly relieved of his saber when he refused to surrender it. The magistrate before whom he was brought declined to hear the case, saying it was a matter for the military, and turned Valiant over to his commanding officer.

Lieutenant H. Eugene Alexander of the Baltimore Battery was assigned to investigate the case. An extensive hearing was held at which over a dozen persons testified. The two privates of Valiant's detail substantiated his account as did five other soldiers who were present in the beer garden at the time of the incident. Officers and men from Battery D testified to Corporal Valiant's good character. The police officers who were involved in the incident all testified that Valiant was drunk and disorderly.

As a result of Lieutenant Alexander's investigation, charges were filed against the Baltimore City Police Department demanding the Sergeant Pryor be discharged from the force. He was not discharged, because the military ultimately withdrew the charges, but he was reprimanded and warned against such action in the future. Lieutenant Richard M. Ray, the senior first lieutenant of Battery D, sent a detail into the city to investigate the incident and was officially reprimanded for unlawfully assuming the prerogative of the Departmental Commander, General Lockwood. The formal reprimand was read before the battery on dress parade where, it seems likely, the sentiments of the battery members were in favor of Lieutenant Ray. Corporal Valiant,

Interior view of Fort C. F. Smith: Battery D served in seven different forts within the Defenses of Washington including Fort C. F. Smith. This photograph shows the variety of ordinance found in the forts around Washington and Baltimore. In the foreground, soldiers drill on a section of field guns. Behind the spectators are three heavier guns "en embrasures." To the right is an 8 inch mortar. A closer inspection reveals a dog standing atop the left caisson and "the daughter of the regiment" standing on the hillside to the right. (*Millers Photographic History*)

thus vindicated, served without further incident until discharged for medical reasons at McKims General Hospital, March 5, 1865.[2]

Shortly after this incident Battery D was assigned to the defenses of Washington. It left by train on the morning of June 6 with its horses but no guns. On its arrival in Washington the horses were turned over to the Quartermaster's Department and the battery marched to Fort Tillinghast, Virginia, near the site of present day Arlington National Cemetery. This was to be the first of numerous duty stations during the remainder of its service. It was attached to the division of Brigadier General Gustavus A. DeRussy in the Twenty-Second Army Corps and served at seven different Virginia forts

Private George Washington Brown: Battery D, First Maryland
Light Artillery. Enlisted March 17, 1864. Mustered out June 24,
1865. (Historical Society of Carroll County)

around the southern perimeter from opposite Georgetown, Maryland, to
Alexandria, Virginia. They were forts Tillinghast, Lyon, Richardson, Ward,
Barnard, and Whipple, the last name being where it spent the longest period.
The entire battery came to Baltimore on a ten day furlough in November of
1864. Battery D returned again to Baltimore at the end of the war where it was
mustered out of the Volunteer Service of the United States on the June 24.[3]

It was not engaged in combat during its term of service. The Confederate attack on Washington in September 1864 was against the northern perimeter of the city, near Silver Spring, Maryland, and Battery D was not involved.

In addition to Captain Bruce, the other officers of Battery D were First Lieutenant Richard M. Ray, age 39, a Baltimore City machinist; First Lieutenant Charles A. Talbott, age 38, an editor; Second Lieutenant George Smith, age 38, a druggist from Albany, New York; and Second Lieutenant Sidney B. Allen, age 28, a railroad man.[4]

All five men were under arrest at various times during the battery's term of service and, during two periods in 1864, three of the five were under arrest simultaneously. Three, including the captain, were dismissed from the service and two returned to duty. In March of 1865 Lieutenant Ray, then in command of the battery, attempted to resign because he was the only officer on duty and found the task of commanding the battery alone to be too great.[5]

Captain Bruce was the first to leave. He was placed under arrest, along with Lieutenant Ray, on June 29, 1864. The charges, which are not stated in the record, must have been trivial because he was released and reinstated to his command a few days later and, on July 9, was serving as field officer of the day. The order reinstating him admonished the arresting officer and instructed him to forward charges in the future to Division Headquarters where the decision would be made as to whether an arrest would be appropriate.[6]

Captain Bruce was called before a board of officers in August of 1864, to examine his "...capacity, qualifications, propriety of conduct and efficiency..." as a battery commander. After inspection of the battery and an extended hearing, the minutes of which are 21 pages in length, the board rendered an unfavorable report. As a result, Captain Bruce was dismissed from volunteer service of the United States by Special Orders Number 340, dated October 10, 1864.[7]

He appealed the decision, submitted a number of impressive testimonials from his former superior officers and others and was granted a new examination. It sustained the original decision and the dismissal was reaffirmed in Special Orders Number 385, dated November 10, 1864.[8]

Lieutenant Talbott was dismissed in January 1865. He was court marshaled and found guilty of "...conduct unbecoming an officer and a gentleman..." and "...conduct prejudicial to good order..." for verbally abusing a fellow officer in the presence of enlisted men. He had been cashiered the previous September for being drunk on duty but his sentence had been remitted "...in view of his previous good character and mitigating circumstances..." and he had been returned to duty.[9]

Lieutenant Smith was also dismissed from the service in January 1865. He was found guilty by court martial of "...conduct unbecoming an officer..." and "...conduct prejudicial to good order..." for playing cards with enlisted men. Lieutenant Smith was the officer who had been the subject of Lieutenant Talbott's ire.[10]

Lieutenant Allen was dismissed from the service March 1865 after being convicted of sleeping while on duty as officer of the day. He was reinstated the same month and remained on active duty for the remainder of the battery's service.[11]

Lieutenant Ray, the senior first lieutenant and acting battery commander after Captain Bruce's departure, was placed under arrest three times during his service with the battery, but each time was ultimately released and returned to duty. The first arrest was that of July 29, 1864, the reason for which is not stated but was probably the same as for Captain Bruce. He was allowed the freedom of the camp. He also was released and returned to duty a short time later and was in command of the battery while Captain Bruce was field officer of the day.

On December 30, 1864 he was again placed under arrest with no reason stated, and was released and returned to duty January 3, 1865. In May he was charged, for trial by court martial, with "...disobedience of [an] order..." and "...being contemptuous and disrespectful toward his commanding officer...." According to the charges he refused to provide his superior with a copy of the battery muster roll and payroll or to let him see it. On being put under arrest he said "Very well Sir I do not mind much. I have got used to being in arrest. This is the third time I have been put into arrest for nothing." Lieutenant Ray was either found not guilty of these charges, received a light sentence or had his conviction remitted; the record does not say. He was not dismissed and continued in command of the battery until it was mustered out on June 24, 1865.[12]

To all whom it may Concern.

Know ye, That *Elias. M. Watson* a Corporal of *Lewt. Richard McRay's* Battery, (*D*,) *1st* Regiment of *Light Arty. Maryland* Volunteers who was enrolled on the *twenty sixth* day of *February* One thousand eight hundred and *sixty four* to serve (3) *three* years or during the war, is hereby **Discharged** from the service of the United States, this *twenty fourth* day of *June*, 1865, at *Baltimore Maryland* by reason of *G. O. No. 105. War Dept. A. G. O. June 2nd 1865*

(*No objection to his being re-enlisted is known to exist.*)

Said *Elias. M. Watson* was born in *Lanchester* in the State of *Pennsylvania* is *twenty three* years of age, *5* feet *5* inches high, *Light* complexion, *Blue* eyes, *Light* hair, and by occupation, when enrolled, a *Farmer*

Given at *Baltimore* this *24"* day of *June 1865.*

*This sentence will be erased should there be anything in the conduct or physical condition of the soldier rendering him unfit for the Army.

G. O. No. 99.]

R.M. Ray. 1st Lieut
Comdg Battery

R.H. Offley
Capt. 1st U.S. infantry
— **Commanding.**
Asst. Comsy. Muster
8" A. Corps

Discharge of Corporal Elias M. Watson: One of the most precious pieces of paper ever held by a soldier, this document states that Corporal Watson enlisted in Battery D, First Maryland Light Artillery on February 26, 1864. It also contains his date and place of birth, occupation, and physical characteristics. Most importantly, it states that his discharge was given in Baltimore on June 24, 1865. (D.C.T.)

THE DEFENSES OF BALTIMORE

THE SECOND MARYLAND LIGHT ARTILLERY

THE FIRST MARYLAND HEAVY ARTILLERY UNITED STATES VOLUNTEERS

The safety of Baltimore was vital to the union cause. Less than fifty miles north of Washington, it was one of the principal population centers of the east. In addition, it was a major logistic and transportation hub of the North, with a large, international seaport, and several railroads running to the north and west. The Baltimore and Ohio Railroad provided the only rail link between Washington, D.C., and the loyal states.[1]

Maryland supplied approximately 46,000 men for the Union war effort. Like the state, Baltimore was deeply divided in its loyalty. In early 1861, both sides were actively recruiting in the city, the Union army on Camden Street near Charles, the Confederates not far distant at Marsh Market. As early as January, 1861, the schooner *Nahant* was entered on the books at the United States Custom House from "the Republic of South Carolina" and in April the bark *Fanny Crenshaw* anchored in Baltimore harbor, flew the Confederate flag.[2]

The first bloodshed of the war occurred on the streets of Baltimore when Southern sympathizers attacked the Sixth Massachusetts infantry changing trains while on its way to the defense of the nation's capital. Three times during the war Confederate armies invaded the North and fought battles not far distant from the city. Two of the largest and bloodiest battles of the war, Antietam in 1862 and Gettysburg in 1863, took place less than 75 miles from Baltimore. In 1864, following the battle of Monocacy just 50 miles from Baltimore, Confederate cavalry raided very close to the city cutting rail and telegraph lines. The gray horsemen proceeded on York Road as far as Govans and burned the home of Governor Augustus Bradford on Charles Street at the site of the present Elk Ridge Country Club.[3]

From the very beginning of hostilities the Federal authorities recognized the importance of establishing adequate protection for the city. John H. Alexander, a renowned Baltimore topographer and scientist, joined the staff of the department commander and assisted in planning the defenses of the city, a vast network of forts surrounding Baltimore. Fort McHenry, at the entrance of the harbor, had been in existence since 1794 as a Regular Army post. A second fort was quickly added on top of Federal Hill overlooking Baltimore's inner harbor and most of the center of the city. Fort Marshall, named for the colonel of the Seventh Maine Infantry which first occupied the site, was east of Patterson Park in what is now the heart of Highlandtown. Fort Worthington guarded the northeast approaches to the city and was located about at the present intersection of Kenwood Avenue and Preston Street. Fort Number One, the first of a series of numbered forts surrounding Baltimore, was situated in Steuart's Grove at what was then the end of West Baltimore Street at its present intersection with Fulton Avenue. Camp Weigel, named for Captain

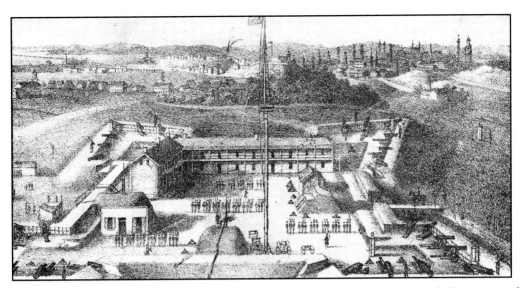

Fort Marshall: Collectively known as The Defenses of Baltimore, Fort Marshall was one of over forty camps and forts built during the war to protect the city. Many of the Maryland regiments and batteries served one or more tours at these forts defending their hometown. (D.C.T.)

William Henry Weigel, Assistant Provost Marshall of Baltimore, was northwest of the city.[4]

All seven of Maryland's Federal artillery units, as well as many from other states, served in the defenses of the city during the course of the war. At various times, Captain Alonzo Snow of Battery B, First Maryland Light Artillery, and Captain Frederic W. Alexander, of the Baltimore Battery of Light Artillery, served as Chief of Artillery of the defenses of Baltimore. Three of the Maryland batteries spent their entire service in the city's defenses and are described in this chapter.[5]

The Second Maryland Light Artillery, United States Volunteers, consisted of two units; Battery A, known as the Junior battery, and Battery B, known as Eagle Battery. They were both mustered into the volunteer service of the United States at Baltimore in July of 1863 for a period of six months.[6]

They were named for two well know Baltimore artillery companies. The original Fells Point Eagle Artillery Company was formed in 1789 and the Junior Artillerists were organized about 1837. Little is known about these originals today other than they apparently existed up until the outbreak of the Civil War. General John R. Kenly once served as a lieutenant in the Eagle Battery and Captain James H. Rigby, commander of Battery A, First Maryland Light Artillery, was also a member of the battery before the war. The order

Wm P Preston Esq.

with the respects

J R Kenly

OUR REPUBLIC:

A LECTURE,

DELIVERED BEFORE THE

EAGLE ARTILLERY,

February 22d, 1844.

BY JOHN R. KENLY, ESQ.

PUBLISHED BY REQUEST.

BALTIMORE:
PRINTED BY JOHN MURPHY
146 MARKET STREET.

"Our Republic": Copy of the lecture John R. Kenly delivered to the Eagle Artillery in 1844. Kenly, a future veteran of the Mexican War, and commander of the Maryland Brigade during the Civil War, presented this copy to William P. Preston. (D.C.T.)

from Thomas Scott, Assistant Secretary of War, establishing Batteries A and B of the Purnell Legion on August 19, 1861, states "… the guns of which are to be produced from Fort McHenry, being those taken from the Junior and Eagle Artillery Companies of Baltimore."[7]

It is possible that the Junior Artillerists and the Eagle Artillery Company were disbanded at the beginning of the war because of the division of sympathies among their members or the general fear that all Baltimore militia companies were pro-Southern.

The Junior Battery was organized at Camp Hoffman in Lafayette Square as was probably the Eagle Battery. From there they moved to Camp Weigel in the northwest defenses of the city. They were under the command of General Erastus B. Tyler in July and August. Defenders' Day 1863 was celebrated in the city with a parade of 1,500 soldiers interspersed with wagons, ambulances, and 125 cavalrymen. The day's festivities concluded with a one hundred gun salute fired by the Junior Artillery at sunset to commemorate the Battle of Fort McHenry in 1814.

In December the Junior and Eagle batteries were twice mentioned in the Official Records as constituting part of the Artillery Reserve of the Eighth Army Corps which was headquartered in Baltimore. Both batteries remained on duty at Camp Weigel until they were mustered out at the end of their term of service in January 1864.[8]

The officers of the Second Maryland Light Artillery were:[9]

Battery A (Junior Artillery)
Captain John M. Bruce
1st Lt. Jacob W. Miller
1st Lt. Richard W. Pryor
2nd Lt. David Duncan
2nd Lt. Richard M. Ray

Battery B (Eagle Artillery)
Captain Joseph H. Audoun
1st Lt. Thomas W. Binyon
1st Lt. Edgar G. Taylor
2nd Lt. Charles H. Dexter
2nd Lt. John H. Jenkins

Sergeant John H. Harvey: Enlisted in the Eagle Artillery on June 25, 1863. Discharged June 16, 1864. (D.C.T.)

Captain Bruce and Lieutenant Ray re-enlisted in February 1864 as officers in Battery D, First Maryland Light Artillery. In December 1863, while still an officer on active duty, Lieutenant Pryor requested a leave of absence because he had been drafted and needed time "...to procure a substitute or make some final arrangements in this matter." His leave was granted and his search for a substitute apparently successful as he was a sergeant in the Baltimore City Police Department in March of 1864 when the incident with Corporal Valiant of Battery D took place. Lieutenant Edgar G. Taylor of the Eagle Battery had previously served in battery A, First Maryland Light Artillery.[10]

Captain Joseph H. Audon had a distinguished civil career. A lawyer by profession, he served successively as Justice of the Peace, Judge and Chief Judge of the Orphan's Court of Baltimore. He was a delegate from Baltimore City to the state constitutional convention in 1864. At the beginning of the war he became active in the Union Relief Association and served on several of its committees, including the "purveyors" committee, which provided meals for members of the armed forces. In addition, he was superintendent of this activity which, in a nine-month period, served 133,000 meals to soldiers in transit through the city. In July 1864, during the threatened Confederate invasion, Judge Audoun was commander of the Second Ward Militia called up to defend the city. He died of a heart attack in 1884, at the age of 61, leaving a wife and seven children.[11]

The First Maryland Heavy Artillery Regiment is the forgotten unit among Maryland artillerists. Mustered in May 1864, it did not complete its organiza-

ARMA PACIS FULCRA

This is to Certify

That *James M. Liews* is an **HONORARY MEMBER** of

THE JUNIOR ARTILLERY,

Company B, First Regiment Light Artillery, attached to the First Light Brigade, Maryland Volunteers.

John M. Bruce Captain.

Francis D. Hetzler J. Secretary.

Baltimore, January 1st 1861.

AMES LUCAS & SON, PRINTERS, BALT.

Membership Certificate: Beautifully illustrated membership certificate given to James M. Liews, an honorary member of The Junior Artillery, in January of 1861. Both the Eagle and Junior batteries were pre-war organizations with strong political affiliations. This document is signed by John M. Bruce, who commanded the wartime battery in 1863. (D.C.T.)

tion, probably for lack of need for heavy artillery regiments that late in the war when heavy artillery regiments were being converted into infantry to reinforce the Army of the Potomac.

The regiment is not mentioned in *The History and Roster of Maryland Volunteers War of 1861-65*, the official record published by the State of Maryland. However, about 100 men were recruited for and served in the First Maryland Heavy Artillery as their records at the Maryland State Archives and the National Archives in Washington attest. The majority were mustered into volunteer service in May of 1864 and the months immediately following. Most were transferred later in 1864 to the First Maryland Potomac Home Brigade (Cole's) Cavalry but, except for fifteen who were not assigned to a specific company, the *History and Roster* does not list their First Maryland Heavy Artillery service.[12]

Captain Frederic W. Alexander was placed on detached service from his own battery in April 1864 to recruit and train the regiment but Company A was the only company organized. The recruiting and training took place during the following months and in July the following order was published.[13]

HDQRS MIDDLE DEPT EIGHTH ARMY CORPS
Baltimore, July 9, 1864

Brig. Gen., J. R. Kenly

....Colonel Jefferies will also give instructions to turn over to you 100 men recruited for Alexander's heavy artillery. They can be used at Fort No. 1 at the guns...

BY COMMAND OF MAJOR GENERAL WALLACE
SAMUEL E. LAWRENCE
ASSISTANT ADJUTANT-GENERAL

Several returns of General Kenly's Third Separate Brigade, Eighth Army Corps, for July show Company A as part of his command. Company A was on duty during the battle of Monocacy and the unsuccessful attack on Washington. Although they were manning one of the forts during the cavalry raid on Baltimore, which was part of that campaign, it is not known if they had

Manning the Big Guns: Heavy artillery regiments were raised to man fortified positions and serve large caliber guns. In this picture a group of soldiers pose around a 32 pound smooth bore cannon mounted on a seacoast carriage. This allowed the weapon to swing in a 180-degree arch. (*Millers Photographic History*)

any direct contact with the raiders.[14]

Only one officer of the First Maryland Heavy Artillery can be positively identified. He was Captain John W. Kraft who was active in recruiting the regiment and who was transferred to Cole's Cavalry on October 8, 1864, where he commanded company H until his muster out of the volunteer service in June of 1865.

Two other officers, listed variously as Lieutenant and Captain, also recruited for the First Maryland Heavy Artillery. They appear in the records of the regiment as R. Cathcart and J. J. Alexander. Cathcart appears to be Captain Robert Cathcart who was recruiting officer for several members of Battery D, Maryland Light Artillery and United States Provost Marshall for the Fourth

Election District of Harford County, Maryland, in 1863. J. J. Alexander is not further identified but could have been a brother of Captain Frederick W. Alexander who had overall responsibility for raising and training the regiment. H. Eugene Alexander, Captain Alexander's brother was a lieutenant in the Baltimore Battery and its captain near the end of its term of service. Neither Cathcart's nor Alexander's names, which are on the manuscript muster rolls, appear in the *History and Roster*, although Kraft's does.[15]

The muster rolls in the Maryland State Archives and some of the Compiled Military Service Records at the national Archives show the age, place of birth and occupation of the recruits. The youngest was seventeen, the oldest, forty-three, with the majority being in their twenties. Five foreign countries were represented in the ranks. Their occupations, probably typical of the volunteer army, included blacksmith, bookbinder, bricklayer, gas fitter, hatter, iron maker, instrument maker, laborer, miner, plumber, plasterer, railroader, sailor, ship sawyer, stone cutter, school teacher, tailor and timekeeper.[16]

The organization seems to have remained intact to the extent that it had been recruited until September 1864 when the men were transferred to Cole's Cavalry, having served approximately five months as Company A, First Maryland Heavy Artillery.

Notes

Civil War Light Artillery

1. Jack Coggin, *Arms and Equipment of the Civil War*, (Garden City, NY: 1962), pp. 61-65; Curt Johnson and Richard C. Anderson , Jr., *Artillery Hell, The Employment of Artillery at Antietam*, (College Station, TX: 1995, pp. 21-25; Frederick W. Wild, *Memoirs and History of Captain F. W. Alexander's Baltimore Battery of Light Artillery*, (Baltimore: 1912, pp. 19-20, 124-125; Francis A. Lord, *Civil War Collector's Encyclopedia*, (New York: 1963), pp. 19,27.

2. Coggins, pp. 67; Johnson and Anderson, pp. 26-27; Lord, p. 24;

3. Coggins, pp. 68, 72-73; Johnson and Anderson, pp. 27-28; John D. Billings, *The History of the Tenth Massachusetts Battery of Light Artillery in the War of the Rebellion*, (Boston: 1909), p. 41.

4. Coggins, pp. 68-69; Johnson and Anderson, p. 27; Lord, p. 47.

5. Coggins, pp. 63,72; Johnson and Anderson, p. 28; Billings, p. 40; *Instructions for Field Artillery, prepared by a Board of Officers*, (Philadelphia,: 1861), Reprinted by Greenwood Press, (New York: 1968), p. 206.

6. Coggins, pp. 63, 70-71,73; Johnson and Anderson, p. 28-29, Billings, pp. 39-42; Instructions for Field Artillery, p. 206.

7. Coggins, pp. 63,71,73; Johnson and Anderson, p. 28.

8. Coggins, pp. 70-71; Johnson and Anderson, pp. 29-30; Billings, pp. 40-41.

9. Coggins, pp. 64-65,71; Johnson and Anderson, p. 29.

10. Coggins, pp. 62,73; Johnson and Anderson, p. 29; Lord, p. 10.

11. Coggins, pp. 62,65; Mark M. Boatner III, *The Civil War Dictionary*, (New York: 1959), p. 120.

The Gist Artillery Battalion

1. Dumas Malone, ed., Dictionary of American Biography, 10 Volumes, (New York: 1934), Vol. VIII, pp. 268-269; The War of the Rebellion: A Compilation of the Official Records of the Union and Confederate Armies, (Washington, D.C.: 1880-1901), 128 Volumes. Series III,

Vol. I, pp. 427,529,578. Hereafter cited as OR. All subsequent citations are from Series I unless otherwise noted.

2. History and Roster of Maryland Volunteers, War of 1861-65, L. Allison Wilmer et al, eds. (Baltimore: 1898), 2 Volumes. Vol. I, p. 460. Hereafter cited as History and Roster; Fredrick Dyer, A Compendium of the War of the Rebellion. (New York: 1959), 3 Volumes. Vol. III, pp. 1230,1231,1237; Major Edward R. Petherbridge, Compiled Military Service Record, National Archives Microfilm Publications, Micro Copy Nr. 384, Compiled Service Records of Volunteer Soldiers Who Served in Organizations from the State of Maryland, Roll 205. Hereafter cited as CMSR; Reiman Steuart, A History of the Maryland Line in the Revolutionary War 1775-1783, (Towson, MD: 1969), p. 85.

3. OR, Vol. 5, pp. 424-437,581,609, 614,616, 620,641.

4. Massachusetts Soldiers, Sailors and Marines in the Civil War, compiled and published by the Adjutant General, (Norwood, MA: 1932), Vol. VI, p. 732; Caroline E. Whitcomb, History of the Second Massachusetts Battery (Nim's Battery) of Light Artillery 1861-1865, (Concord, NH: No Date), p 15; OR, Vol. 11, Part II, p.239.

5. OR, Vol. 5, pp. 424-437, contains an extensive correspondence between Generals Dix and Lockwood concerning the purposes and progress of the operation. Dyer, Vol. III, pp. 1230-1231; Batteries A and B Maryland Light Artillery, Record of Events, CMSR, Roll 45.

6. "Three Civil War Letters of James H. Rigby: A Maryland Federal Artillery Officer", Maryland Historical Magazine, Vol. 57, (1962), p. 156. Hereafter cited as MHM.

7. Colonel William H. Purnell, CMSR, Roll 205; Record Group 94, Records of Adjutant General's Office, Volunteer Service Division Files p. 71 (vs) 1862, 9w3 21/19/D, Box 116, Military Reference Branch (NNRM) Textual Reference Division, National Archives, Washington, D.C.

8. Major Petherbridge, CMSR and Pension File, Application Nr. 779846, Certificate Nr. 682482, National Archives, Washington, D.C.; OR, Vol. 11, Part I, p. 353, Part II, p. 239.

9. Major Petherbridge, CMSR and Pension File; J. Thomas Scharf, History of Baltimore City and County, (Baltimore, 1971) reprint of 1881 edition, 2 Volumes, Vol. I, pp. 250,132,140; OR, Vol. 37, Part I pp. 296, 326,358, 399.

10. Francis H. Brown, Harvard University in the War of 1861- 1865, (Boston: 1886), p. 158; Bigelow Family Papers, ms, N-195, Box 7, Massachusetts Historical Society, Boston, Massachusetts

Battery A First Maryland Artillery

1. History and Roster, pp. 796-798; Dyer, Volume III, pp. 1230-1231.
2. Dyer, Vol. III, p 1230; Rigby Letters, MHM, P 156.
3. Dyer, Volume III, p. 1230; OR: Volume 11, Part II, pp. 265-266, 238-239. Principal source is Captain Wolcott's report, July 5, 1862.
4. OR, Vol. 11, Part II, pp. 33,266,325.
5. Report of Lieutenant Samuel L. Benjamin Battery E, 2nd U.S. Artillery, September 3, 1862 in Civil War Times Illustrated, March/April, 1993, p 22; Grave Stone, Old National Cemetery, Baltimore, Maryland.
6. Rigby Letters, MHM, P 157; OR: Vol. 19, Part I, pp. 375,380.
7. OR, Vol. 19, Part I pp. 381-382; Position Markers, Cope Time and Position Maps, Antietam National Battlefield, Sharpsburg, Maryland; J. Thomas Scharf, History of Maryland, (Hatsboro, PA: 1967), Reprint of the 1879 edition, 3 Volumes, Volume III, p. 487.
8. Rigby Letters, MHS, P 158.
9. John Michael Priest, Antietam, the Soldiers Battle, (Shippensburg, PA: 1989), pp. 295-296.
10. Unidentified Newspaper Clipping, Bigelow Papers, Massachusetts Historical Society ; OR: Vol. 19 Part I, p. 382.
11. Rigby Letters, MHS, p. 158; OR: Vol. 19, Part I p. 195. The original issue of artillery caps had a scarlet top. Most men converted to the less conspicuous all blue caps but, according to family tradition, Sergeant Marsden did not. His made a perfect target for Confederate sharpshooters.
12. OR: Vol. 21, pp. 181-187,214, 525-526; Rigby Letters, MHS, p. 159; OR, Vol. 21, pp. 458-460, 463.
13. Rigby Letters, MHS, p. 159.
14. OR, Vol. 25, Part I pp. 596-597.
15. OR, Vol. 25, pp. 596,246,250,563,593.
16. OR, Vol. 25, Part I pp. 567-568,595-596.
17. OR, Vol. 25, Part I, pp. 596-597,563-566, 601.
18. OR, Vol. 25, Part I, pp. 597,601.
19. OR, Vol. 25, Part II, pp. 471-472.
20. OR, Vol. 27, Part I, p. 899; OR, Vol. 27, Part I, pp. 896,872-873.
21. OR, Vol. 27, Part I, p 899; The report of the State of Maryland Gettysburg Monument Commission to His Excellency E. E. Jackson, Governor of Maryland, June 17, 1891, p. 35.
22. OR, Vol. 29, Part I pp. 129, 225; Captain James H. Rigby, CMSR, Roll 49; OR, Vol. 29, Part I, p.668.
23. Boatner, pp. 81,552; OR, Vol. 29, Part I, p. 225,668; OR, Vol. 33, p. 114.

24. OR, Vol. 33, p. 1047; Vol. 37, Part I pp. 570, 700; Vol. 40, Part II, p. 492; Vol. 37, Part II pp. 14, 548; Vol. 43, p. 775; Vol. 46, Part II, p. 761; Dyer, Vol. III, p. 1230.

25. History and Roster, p. 795; Dyer, Volume III, p. 1230.

26. Massachusetts Soldiers, Sailors and Marines in the Civil War, Vol. VI, p. 732; Whitcomb, p 15; Vital Records of Roxbury, Massachusetts, Vol. I-Births (Salem, MA: 1925), p 348; Mrs. Wolcott to Lt. John Bigelow, October 2, 1862, Bigelow Papers, Massachusetts Historical Society; Captain John W. Wolcott, CMSR, Roll 51; History and Roster, pp. 795-796; Flag Collection, Maryland State Archives, Maryland.

27. Rigby Letters, MHS, p. 155, Captain James Rigby, CMSR, Roll 49; also his Pension File, Application Nr. 673729, Certificate Nr. 437824, National Archives, Washington, D.C.; History and Roster, p. 797; Grave Stone, Old National Cemetery, Baltimore, Maryland.

28. Dyer, Volume III, p. 1231; Flag Collection, Maryland State Archives.

Battery B First Maryland Light Artillery

1. History and Roster, p. 802; Dyer, Volume III, p. 1231; Morton F. Taylor, Sketch of Snow's Battery, typescript, n.d., Historical Society of Cecil County, Elkton, MD.

2. History and Roster, p. 802; Dyer, Volume III, p. 1231; Boatner, pp. 632-634; Scharf, History of Maryland, Vol. III, p. 487.

3. OR, Vol. 11, Part I, pp. 353,1001.

4. OR, Vol. 11, Part I, pp. 1001-1003.

5. OR, Vol. 11, Part I, p. 354.

6. Boatner, pp. 504,507.

7. OR, Vol. 11, Part I, pp. 238,239,267,268.

8. Boatner, pp. 17-21; OR, Vol. 19, Part I, pp. 401-404.

9. OR, Vol. 19, Part I, pp. 404-405.

10. Lt. Theodore J. Vanneman's letter to his wife, September 13, 1862. Copy at Headquarters, Antietam National Battlefield, Sharpsburg, MD, courtesy of his grandson, Samuel Vanneman.

11. Boatner, pp. 310-313; OR, Vol. 21, Part I, pp. 524,525,530. Diary of Captain Alonzo Snow, December 13, 1862, unpaged, in his Pension File, Application Nr. 427345, Certificate Nr. 277477, National Archives, Washington D.C.

12. Boatner, pp. 136-140; OR, Vol. 25, Part II, p. 119ff.

13. OR, Vol. 25, Part I, p. 156, Part II, pp. 587,575: Snow Diary March 30-June 3, 1863.

14. Snow's Diary, June 25-July 3, 1863; OR, Vol. 27, Part III, pp. 314-315,440,547,635.

15. OR, Vol. 27, Part III, pp. 639,679,726,813; Vol. 29, Part II, pp. 139,615; Vol. 33, pp. 480,894; Snow's Dairy, July 6- September 21, 1863, May 5, 1864.

16. Laura Virginia Hale, Four Valiant Years in the Lower Shenandoah Valley 1861-1865 (Front Royal, 1986), pp. 358, 362.

17 Boatner, p. 588; OR, Vol. 37, Part I, pp. 76,77,79-81,82; Franz Sigel, "Sigel On the Shenandoah Valley in 1864," Battles and Leaders of the Civil War, 4 Volumes, (New York: 1884-1887), Vol. IV, pp. 489-490; Snow's Diary, May 14-15, 31, 1864.

18. Snow's Diary, May 30, 1864.

19. OR, Vol. 37, Part I, pp. 94-95; Snow's Dairy, May 23, June 5, 1864; Boatner, pp. 497,652-653.

20. OR, Vol. 37, Part I, pp. 99-100; Snow's Dairy, June 5-16, 1864; Boatner, pp. 497,652-653.

21. OR, Vol. 37, Part I, p. 101; Snow's Dairy, June 21, 22, 1864; Taylor; CMSRs of Privates Brown, Buckley, Reed, Simmers, Van Court and Williams, Rolls 46, 49, 50, 51.

22. OR, Vol. 37, Part I, p. 103, Part II, pp. 760-761: Snow's Dairy, June 23-July 10, 1864; OR, Vol. 46, Part III, p. 1046.

23. OR, Vol. 37, Part I pp. 188-189; Snow's Dairy, July 28-August 3, 1864.

24. Snow's Dairy, November 8, 1864.

25. History and Roster, p. 802.

26. Alonzo Snow's Regular Army record, Micro Copy Nr. 233, Register of Enlistments in the U.S. Army 1789-1914, Vol. 38, p. 171, Entry 115, National Archives, Washington, D.C.; Captain Snow's Civil War CMSR, Roll 50 and Pension file.

27. Taylor; Cecil Whig, Elkton, MD, October 11, 1890, November 24, 1939; Cecil Democrat, Elkton, MD, November 25, 1939, Historical Society of Cecil County.

Baltimore Battery Endnotes

1. Captain John M. Bruce, CMSR Roll 46; History and Roster, p. 811; Dyer, Vol. III, p. 1231; Battery D Record of Events, Roll 45; OR, Vol. 33, p. 1051.

2. Corporal James B. Valiant, CMSR, Roll 50; Lieutenant Richard M. Ray. CMSR, Roll 49.

3. Battery D Records of Events, CMSR, Roll 45; Battery D Regimental

Records, ms, Morning Reports, Order Book, Military Reference Branch (NNRM) Textual Reference Division, National Archives, Washington, D.C. Hereafter cited as MR and OB; *OR*, Vol. 36, Part III, p. 634; Vol. 37, Part I, p. 700, Part II, pp. 543-546.

4. Battery D Muster Rolls, ms, Maryland State Archives, Annapolis, MD. Identification numbers S936-39; 50,055-39; 2/6/3/21 and S936-41; 50, 055-41; 2/5/4/39.

5. The facts concerning the difficulties of the officers of Battery D are found primarily in their Compiled Military Service Records. Some additional details are from the Morning Reports and Order Books cited in note 4. There are also references in the manuscript muster rolls at the Maryland State Archives.

6. Captain John M. Bruce, CMSR, Roll 46; MR and OB.

7. Case of Captain John M. Bruce, Record Group 94, Records of Adjutant General's Office, Volunteer Service Division Files W2469 (vs) 1864, 9w3 20/16/c Box 655, Military References Branch (NNRM) Textual Reference Division, National Archives, Washington D.C.

8. Special Orders Number 385, November 10, 1864, Records of the Adjutant General in Special Orders Books (bound volumes), Volume IV, Orders 327-478, Military Reference Branch (NNRM) Textual Reference Division, National Archives, Washington, D.C.

9. Lieutenant Charles A. Talbott, CMSR, Roll 50; MR and OB.

10. Lieutenant George Smith, CMSR, Roll 50; MR.

11. Lieutenant Sidney B. Allen, CMSR, Roll 45, MR and OB.

12. Lieutenant Richard M. Ray, CMSR, Roll 49, MR and OB.

The Defenses of Baltimore Endnotes

1. Baltimore during the Civil War is well treated in various histories. See, Daniel Carroll Toomey, The Civil War in Maryland, (Baltimore: 1989), J. Thomas Scharf, History of Baltimore City and County, previously cited, and Scott Sumpter Sheads and Daniel Carroll Toomey, Baltimore During the Civil War, (Linthicum, MD: 1997).

2. Francis Trevelyan Miller, Ed. ,Photographic History of the Civil War, (New York: 1912), 10 Volumes, Vol. 10, p.146; Scharf, History of Baltimore City and County, Vol. I, p. 129.

3. Boatner, pp. 42,17,334,561. For a detailed account of the Confederate raid on Baltimore see Charles A. Earp, "War Came to Town 125 Years Ago," The Towson Times, July 12, 1989, pp. 32-33.

4. John L. Blecker, manuscript biography of John Henry Alexander,

Diehlman-Hayward Genealogy File, Maryland Historical Society. Scharf, History of Baltimore City and County, Vol. I, pp. 131-132,184; Baltimore During the Civil War, The Peale Museum, (Baltimore: n.d.) includes prints of various military installations throughout the city, Baltimore News-Post, November 15, 1943.

5. See chapters on these batteries for further information on Snow's and Alexander's service as Chiefs of Artillery of the Baltimore defenses. Snow also refers to it in his diary.

6. Dyer, Vol. I, p. 154; History and Roster, pp. 825, 829.

7. Scharf, History of Maryland, Vol. III, p. 669; Scharf, History of Baltimore City and County, Vol. I, pp. 133-134; Captain James H. Rigby, pension file; OR, Series III, Vol. I, p. 427.

8. OR, Vol. 27, Part III, p. 810; Vol. 29, Part II, pp. 134,168,611; CMSRs of Lieutenant Richard W. Pryor (Junior Battery), Captain Joseph H. Audoun (Eagle Battery). Private George Zerkle (Eagle Battery), roll 45.

9. Election of Officers, Eagle Battery, June 24, 1863; Junior Battery, July 7, 1863, ms, S936-41, 50, 055-41 2/5/4/39, Maryland State Archives; History and Roster, Volume I, pp. 825,829; Dyer, Vol. I, p. 154.

10. Lieutenant Richard W. Pryor, CMSR, Roll 45; History and Roster, pp. 795-796.

11. Scharf, History of Baltimore City and County, Volume I, pp. 152-153; Vol. II, p. 728; Scharf, History of Maryland, Vol. III, pp. 632,751; Baltimore City Directory, 1865-66, Diehlman-Hayward genealogy File; obituary, The Baltimore Sun, August 25, 1884.

12. Dyer, Vol. III, p. 1231; First Maryland Heavy Artillery muster rolls, S936-41, 50055-41, 2/5/4/39, Maryland State Archives; First Maryland Heavy Artillery CMSRs roll 51; History and Roster, p. 700.

13. Captain F. W. Alexander, CMSR, Roll 43; Dyer, Vol. III, p. 1231; OR, Vol. 37, Part II, p. 147.

14. OR, Vol. 37, Part II, pp. 218,252,298.

15. History and Roster, p. 688; Private Stevenson Price, CMSR, Roll 49; William R. Hudgins ND George Smith, Battery D morning reports, mss, National Archives; Scharf, History of Maryland, Vol. III, p. 554.

16. Muster Rolls, ms, Maryland State Archives; CMSRs, Roll 51, National Archives.

THE CAVALRY

BY

DANIEL CARROLL TOOMEY

Dedicated to my friend and co-author,
Charles Albert Earp.
He knew them as a boy and
loved them as a man.
"All for the Union"

CONTENTS

INTRODUCTION

When the call went out for volunteers after the firing on Fort Sumter, General Winfield Scott, ranking general in the Regular Army and defacto commander of all volunteer forces, decreed that no cavalry regiments were to be accepted into the service. The reason for this was the fact that the personnel and equipment required to put a regiment in the field was considerably more expensive than that of an infantry regiment. Cavalry officers drew a higher pay scale and the number of technically skilled personnel—blacksmiths and saddlers, mobile forges and, of course, the horses, drove the cost of a fully equipped mounted regiment to $500,000 in 1861. To go with this was the theory that a cavalry regiment could not be equipped and trained before the supposed 90-day war was over. It was not until August of 1861, that a Maryland cavalry regiment began to recruit in the state. By the end of the war four regiments and four independent companies were credited to the state's enlistment quotas. All but one of these, the Third Maryland Cavalry Regiment, served in the East.[1]

At the beginning of the war a volunteer cavalry regiment was given the same table of organization as its pre-war Regular Army counter part. As with all branches of the service, new weapons and tactics dictated change. By 1863 the composition of a cavalry regiment was set forth in Special Order No. 110. It consisted of a regimental staff and twelve companies called troops. The companies were divided into three battalions, each commanded by a major. Each battalion was a self-contained unit, allowing the regiment to operate as a whole or dispersed over a wide area with multiple functions. Its table of organization was as follows:

Regiment of Cavalry (twelve companies)

1 Colonel	1 Regimental Commissary (extra Lt.)
1 Lieutenant Colonel	1 Chaplain
3 Majors	1 Veterinary Surgeon
1 Surgeon	1 Sergeant Major
2 Assistant Surgeons	1 Quartermaster Sergeant
1 Regimental Adjutant (extra Lt.)	1 Commissary Sergeant
1 Regimental Quartermaster (extra Lt.)	2 Hospital Stewards
1 Chief Trumpeter	1 Saddler Sergeant

Company or Troop

1 Captain	5 Sergeants
1 First Lieutenant	8 Corporals
1 Second Lieutenant	2 Trumpeters
1 First Sergeant	2 Farriers or Blacksmiths
1 Quartermaster Sergeant	1 Saddler
1 Commissary Sergeant	1 Wagoner
60 to 78 Privates[2]	

During the first two years of the war, the Union Cavalry was out classed by its Southern rivals in all categories: leadership, horsemanship, organization, and quality of mounts. The First Regiment and the original four companies of Cole's Cavalry suffered through all the growing pains of the Federal cavalry. When General George B. McClellan first organized the Army of the Potomac its basic formation was that of the infantry division with cavalry and artillery units assigned to each division. This diluted the effectiveness of both of these branches of service until later in the war.[3]

General John Pope and his short-lived Army of Virginia took the first step towards improving the Union Cavalry. Special Order #45 placed the cavalry of each corps under a Chief of Cavalry and ordered all detached men to report to their regiments for assignments by the cavalry commander of their respective corps. This was the first time many of the regiments were actually together in the field as a single unit, let alone anything approaching the brigade size units that J.E.B. Stuart flung against the Union armies in Virginia. As early as October of 1861 the Confederate War department ordered the cavalry regiments in Virginia brigaded under the command of newly promoted General J. E. B. Stuart. One year later Stuart was a major general with a division of cavalry and five batteries of horse artillery.[4]

The Union cavalry moved ever so slowly towards its destiny in 1862 when General McClellan, back for a second chance at commanding the Army of the Potomac, gave General Alfred Pleasonton a division of cavalry consisting of five brigades. Just prior to the Battle of Fredericksburg, Pleasonton pushed for the creation of a corps of cavalry complete with eight batteries of horse artillery. When General Joseph Hooker took command of the Army of the Potomac after the debacle at Fredericksburg, he replaced Pleasonton with

Major General Alfred Pleasonton: A native of
Washington, D.C., he commanded the Cavalry Corps
of the Army of the Potomac at the Battle of Brandy
Station and during the Gettysburg Campaign.
(D.C.T.)

General Stoneman. The new cavalry commander organized his corps into
three divisions and a reserve brigade. Again all squadrons, companies, and
detachments were ordered to report to their assigned brigades for orders ema-
nating from their division commanders. No longer would the Union cavalry
be errant boys for the infantry. Stoneman led his new command on its first
great offensive undertaking during the Chancellorsville Campaign. Despite
some success during "Stoneman's Raid," which the First Maryland participated in, he was replaced by General Alfred Pleasonton on May 22.[5]

Whether it was apparent to all concerned or not, the Cavalry Corps of the Army of the Potomac pulled even with its adversary in the Army of Northern Virginia on the morning of June 9, 1863, when it splashed across the Rappahannock River in a surprise attack that became known as the Battle of Brandy Station. Variously described as a draw and a Southern victory, one of Stuart's staff officers, Major H. B. McClellan, summed it up best. "One result of incalculable importance certainly did follow this battle—it made the Federal cavalry." Within a month's time the Union cavalry would again confront Stuart's horsemen. General David Gregg's division supported by Custer's Brigade turned backed Stuart's attack on the third day at Gettysburg. The First Maryland Regiment and Company A of the Purnell Legion were there. The Union cavalry now had the skill, horses, and equipment, but still lacked leadership at the top command position. This would come in 1864 when Grant brought General Phillip Sheridan east to command the Union cavalry. From Gettysburg to Appomattox, the Cavalry Corps of the Army of the Potomac would contribute its full share to the final Union victory.[6]

FIRST MARYLAND CAVALRY REGIMENT

Failing to win a three-month war, both governments set about to create a fully organized and long standing army. The prohibition against cavalry units was dropped and each state remaining in the Union was authorized to raise mounted commands as well as infantry and artillery. The First Maryland Regiment had to overcome all the difficulties inherent to the recruiting of early war regiments and suffered from the misuse of the cavalry arm in the Army of the Potomac during the first two years of the conflict.

The First Maryland Regiment began to enlist recruits during the summer of 1861. Companies H and I were raised in Washington and Allegheny counties. They saw service during Jackson's Romney Campaign and the attack on Hancock before ever joining the regiment in Baltimore.[1]

The state governments did not always appreciate the sense of urgency in bringing units to full strength. Numerous commands lingered through the winter months of 1861 before the required number of men were secured for muster into Federal service. On January 16, 1862, Adjutant General Lorenzo Thomas wrote Governor Bradford a letter suggesting that the four companies of cavalry presently stationed in Western Maryland be combined with the six in Baltimore City to form a complete regiment under the command of

Lieutenant Colonel Andrew G. Miller, "…an old regular officer of known ability and experience." This was accomplished in March and the entire regiment trained at Camp Carroll until May of 1862. It was a mixed lot. Companies A through E were from Baltimore City; F from Cockeysville and Baltimore; G and K from Pittsburgh; H and I Western Maryland; and L and M from Washington, DC. Andrew Miller was promoted to full colonel on May 2, but never took the field with his command. His resignation on May 22 was possibly caused by a severe injury to his right arm, which he suffered while loading his troops on the train for Winchester.[2]

In May the regiment was shipped by rail to Harper's Ferry. The First Battalion under Lieutenant Colonel Charles Wetschky (Companies A, B, C, G, I) was ordered to join General Bank's division at Winchester where it began to learn the art of picket and outpost duty on May 20. Two days later the Battalion was sent out six miles on the road from Strasburg to cover a retreating wagon train. In the skirmish it recaptured a hospital wagon. Returning to camp it spent a sleepless night filled with false alarms. The next day it was sent out on the road to Romney and bivouacked for the night three miles from Winchester. On May 24 Jackson's army recaptured the town and the Marylanders lost all the equipment and supplies in their main camp. Company A alone lost 14 saddles, 24 bridles, 12 pistols, 36 overcoats, 98 pairs of pants, 98 cavalry jackets, 27 pairs of shoes, 37 caps, and 50 pairs of highly useful shoulder scales, along with all their tents and cooking utensils. Company B lost their blacksmith's forge.

In the retreat from Winchester to the Potomac River the Battalion formed a rear guard with Donnelly's infantry brigade and collected about 50 Union stragglers. When it reached the river it crossed on a ferry above Dam #4 and marched cross country to Williamsport.[3]

The Second Battalion under Major James M. Deems (companies D, F, H, K, L) arrived at Harper's Ferry on May 25 and were employed in the defense of that post. Major Deems ordered Company L, The Putnam Rangers, under Captain George Thistleton, to scout the approaches to Harper's Ferry. The Rangers moved so close to a Rebel battery that they were able to knock one of its drivers off his horse with carbine fire. The battery then opened on the Union cavalry with shell and round shot. For his bravery in this action Sergeant James M. Johnson was brevetted a second lieutenant.[4]

Following his success at Winchester, Stonewall Jackson ordered General Charles Winder to take the Stonewall Brigade and capture Harper's Ferry. Winder's advance on the 28th was disrupted near Charlestown by a stubborn Union resistance. He then deployed his infantry and pushed the Union forces as far as Hall Town. The next day Jackson arrived at the head of his army with the intention of attacking Harper's Ferry, but learning of the presence of Shields' and Fremont's armies 50 miles in his rear was forced to order a retreat. In the action near Charlestown, the second battalion had 1 captain, 8 privates, and 10 horses captured by the Stonewall Brigade.[5]

In June the two battalions were united for the first time in the field and assigned to the brigade commanded by General Hatch and sta-

Sergeant Henry Glunt: Enlisted as a private in Company G, First Maryland Cavalry on August 25, 1861. Discharged November 11, 1864. (D.C.T.)

tioned at Fairfax, Virginia. It was constantly engaged in scouting, picketing, and formed part of Hatch's reconnaissance to Madison Court House and the Luray Valley. On July 13 a portion of the command burned bridges on the Rapidan River.[6]

Although officially consolidated, the various dispositions of the First Maryland during the summer of 1862 illustrate the fact that the Union Army had not yet learned how to utilize its cavalry. In July Company A was detailed as bodyguard for General Christopher C. Augur. Company C was assigned for special duty with General Bank's Corps and stationed at Langley. The captain of Company F with 5 sergeants, 4 corporals, and 10 privates were on detached service. Companies H and I were stationed at Harper's Ferry until September.

Company L served as a bodyguard for General Franz Siegel during the month of June. Throughout the Army of the Potomac, cavalry regiments were often little more than playthings for brigade and division commanders who could not understand why J.E.B. Stuart's cavalry continued to best their own mounted arm.[7]

During the months of June and July the men of the First Maryland were constantly in the saddle. On June 4 Company B was assigned to the Fifth New York Cavalry during the occupation of Martinsburg and Winchester. Twenty men from Company A were sent from Little Washington to Front Royal on July 24 to escort a courier. Six miles east of Front Royal they were attacked by Rebel cavalry. Sergeant Thomas Hughs, Corporal David Bennett, and five privates were captured along with ten horses. In a skirmish at Madison Court House on August 8, Company B lost five men wounded and 7 taken prisoner. Company I captured 5 of the enemy and helped burn the railroad bridge over the Rapidan River. In another skirmish they recaptured 36 men from the Third District of Columbia Regiment. Company L was also at Madison Court House where it lost 2 men killed and had 5 others captured. Company G was surprised by the enemy while scouting near Madison Mills and lost 4 enlisted men killed and seven captured along with its captain. When ordered to retreat from the Rapidan at the end of August, Company K was forced to abandon 15 horses, which were completely broken down from continuous hard service.[8]

The month of August 1862 ended with the Second Battle of Bull Run. The wreckage of General John Pope's Army of Virginia fled back to the safety of the Nation's Capitol. This opened the way for Lee's first attempt to invade Pennsylvania. A major stumbling block to Lee's northward advance was the garrison of nearly 12,000 men at Harper's Ferry commanded by a Regular Army officer from Maryland, Colonel Dixon S. Miles. Impossible to defend once the high ground was taken around the town, it was equally impossible for Lee to leave such a large force astride his line of communication between Maryland and Virginia. All of this eventually led to the Battle of Sharpsburg on September 17, 1862.

Lee's army crossed the Potomac above and below Harper's Ferry and stopped at Frederick City where he issued orders for its capture. Companies H and I were part of the doomed garrison. On September 8 Captain Charles H. Russell led 50 men from Company I on a reconnaissance from Maryland

Heights toward Frederick City. At Petersville they captured a Rebel spy. The next day the Sergeant Major of the Twelfth Louisiana Infantry fell into their hands at the town of Jefferson. From Jefferson they road cross country and struck the National Pike 3 miles west of Frederick where they overran a Rebel picket post and captured 13 men and 9 horses. Among the prisoners were two deserters from Company H of the First Maryland.[9]

As the trap closed on Harper's Ferry companies H and I fought with other units in the garrison to defend Maryland Heights on September 12. Private Matthew T. McClannahn of Company I wrote after the war, "I lost my partner P. L. Hiteschew who was shot in the left thigh…" After turning his friend over to a surgeon in an Ohio regiment he carried four more wounded men to safety before the Heights were evacuated. One of these was his friend's brother, Lieutenant Daniel C. Hiteschew, from Company H who was also shot in the hip and died a few days later. Sergeant Phillip Hiteschew recovered from his wound and rose to the rank of captain of his company.[10]

On the night of September 13 Colonel Miles ordered Captain Russell to take a few men from Company I, sneak through the Confederate lines, and report the condition of the garrison to General McClellen. Russell and five men left after dark that night. They moved up the Virginia side of the Potomac River and crossed into Maryland at the mouth of the Monocacy River where they captured a Rebel picket post. Realizing that speed was all important to their mission, Russell had the prisoners tied and gagged and then headed for Frederick City which he reached early the next morning and reported in person to General McClellen.[11]

Besides the two companies from the First Maryland at Harper's Ferry there were other regiments and detachments of cavalry numbering about 1500 men and horses. The latter were sorely needed by the Confederates. As the noose tightened around their position, the Union cavalry commanders pressed Colonel Miles for permission to try an escape. This was eventually granted and the whole mounted force crossed the pontoon bridge into Maryland on the night of September 14 and escaped by way of the Sharpsburg Road. Companies H and I assisted in the capture of General Longstreet's reserve ammunition train, which the column encountered in route to Greencastle, Pennsylvania.[12]

After the Battle of Antietam Federal forces, including the newly formed Maryland Brigade under General Kenly, reoccupied Harper's Ferry.

Companies H and I were assigned to this command. Fifty men from these companies were the only cavalry to accompany General John W. Geary on a reconnaissance in force toward Winchester on December 2. After a skirmish with two companies of the Twelfth Virginia Cavalry at Charlestown, the column continued on the Berryville road until within one mile of that town where it encountered the Seventh and Twelfth Virginia cavalry regiments. These were shelled out of their position by the guns of Knap's Battery. The enemy retreated in the direction of Winchester followed by the Maryland cavalry. The Twelfth Virginia turned on the Marylanders and chased them back on their main body of troops. Knap's gunners and the Seventh Ohio Infantry waited until the charging Rebels were within 100 yards of their position and then opened a devastating fire that killed or wounded about 25 men and several horses. The town of Winchester was occupied on December 4.[13]

The last action of the year for the First Maryland Regiment came on December 27 near Dumfries, Virginia. When Rebel cavalry captured a Union patrol on the Telegraph Road, Colonel Charles Candy, the post commander at Dumfries, ordered Captain Joseph H. Cook of Company L to locate the enemy and recapture the Union prisoners if possible. Cook's detachment struck an enemy skirmish line near a mill on the Quantico Creek where the capture had taken place. The unexpected fire wounded several horses and caused some confusion in the ranks. Cook fell back to the protection of a Union battery and covered its flank until the action was over. Colonel Candy commended him in his after action report.[14]

After a disastrous defeat at Fredericksburg in December of 1862, morale in the Army of the Potomac was at an all time low. General Ambrose E. Burnside was replaced by "Fighting Joe" Hooker early in 1863. Hooker not only reorganized the infantry divisions of the army, he created a cavalry corps consisting of three divisions and a reserve brigade. The commander of this new mounted force was Brigadier General Alfred Pleasonton. Special Order No. 4 issued from the cavalry corps headquarters on February 12, assigned the First Maryland to the Third Division commanded by Brigadier General David McMurtrie Gregg. Colonel Van Keilmansegge was in command of the regiment at this time. He had joined the regiment at Hall's Farm in October of 1862. The brigade was now at Camp Bayard near Belle Plain, Virginia. Four days later General Gregg organized his division into two brigades. Colonel

Cavalryman's greatcoat: worn by Private Andrew Snyder. Snyder was a resident of Four Locks when he enlisted at Williamsport on December 17, 1862. He served in Company I of the First Maryland Regiment until his discharge on August 8, 1865. Private Snyder died on March 20, 1916, and is buried in Rose Hill Cemetery, Hagerstown, Maryland.

A cavalry coat differs from the infantry model in that it has a double row of buttons on the breast and the cape extends down as far as the cuff on the coat sleeve. This one is unique in that the standard issued "Eagle" buttons have been replaced with Maryland State Seal buttons. (D.C.T.)

Keilmansegge was given command of the Second Brigade, which consisted of the First Maryland, First New Jersey, and First Pennsylvania Regiments. Lieutenant Colonel James M. Deems temporarily commanded the regiment.

While at Camp Bayard Colonel Von Keilmansgge requested a ten-day leave of absence on March 18. "Letters received from relatives in Europe require my presence at New York to make some arrangements with the Consul General of Hanover…" General Gregg approved his request the next day. In May it was learned that Von Keilmansgge had been dismissed from the service for being A.W.O.L while serving the Fourth Missouri Cavalry Regiment. He was dismissed again on May 14 by Special Order No. 215. Lieutenant Colonel Deems continued to command the regiment.[15]

In April of 1863 the Cavalry Corps of the Army of the Potomac launched its first full-scale operation with nearly 10,000 troopers—unprecedented numbers prior to this time during the war. Hooker hoped to launch the raid two weeks prior to his crossing the Rappahannock River with the main army and cause havoc with Lee's supply lines. Rain delayed their departure for two weeks forcing them to cross the river in tandem with the infantry on April 29. The First Maryland was with the divisions that struck the Richmond, Fredericksburg, and Potomac Railroad. Some damage was done, but "Stoneman's Raid" was deemed a failure. Its singular value was to cause a change of personnel in command positions, which was what the Union Cavalry needed most of all—leadership.[16]

On June 9 the greatest cavalry battle ever fought in North America took place at Brandy Station and the First Maryland played a conspicuous part in the action. General Hooker's intelligence sources informed him in May of 1863 that Lee was planing a second invasion of the North. He ordered General Pleasonton to take his Cavalry Corps supported by two brigades of infantry and Battery K of the First U.S. Artillery across the Rappahannock River and make a reconnaissance in force toward Culpeper, Virginia. His mission was to discover the position and direction of the Army of Northern Virginia.[17]

The Union cavalry crossed the river under the cover of a heavy morning fog at Beverly and Kelly's fords. Surprised Johnny Rebs scrambled to fight a delaying action as couriers raced off to sound the alarm. The Second Brigade was now under the command of Colonel Percy Wyndham. When a strong enemy force was encountered about mid morning he ordered a section of artillery forward supported by the First Maryland. Major Charles Russell, former captain of Company I, led his battalion in a charge that drove the enemy down the Culpeper Road and captured an ambulance containing General Stuart's headquarters papers and instructions for the up coming campaign. The Confederates then brought up two regiments and attempted to push the Marylanders back. One officer after the other fell from his horse leading counter charges by the First Maryland. Lieutenant Robert J. Kimble led Company I eight times back into the fight after Captain Francis M. Kreager was wounded.

In the ebb and flow of the battle the combat varied from massed battalions to small unit actions. Men on both sides found themselves surrounded and escaping almost at will. Sergeant Charles U. Embery of Company I was mistaken for a Rebel because of the brown blouse he wore. He served as an orderly for a Confederate officer until he had the opportunity to escape. Captain John K. Buckley was taken prisoner three times before making his escape permanent. Major Russell found himself in the rear of the Confederate lines with only 15 men. Through a series of bluffs and charges he regained the Union lines with his men and 14 prisoners.[18]

As the day wore on Stuart brought more and more of his Cavalry regiments into the fight and summoned infantry support. Having secured the necessary intelligence and damaged Stuart in both his manpower and prestige. Pleasonton wisely retreated back across the river. As the sun went down on that June day J.E.B. Stuart held the battlefield, but he had lost his air of invincibility. Gettysburg would prove that to be a fact.

The First Maryland suffered many casualties at the Battle of Brandy Station, but it had given at least as good as it got, having captured one ambulance, one battle flag, and Company I having burned the train station there. Gregg's Third Division captured a total of 8 Confederate officers and 107 enlisted men with many others killed or wounded.

The First Maryland re-crossed the Rappahannock River at Beverly Ford and went into camp at Warrenton Junction for a brief and well-earned rest. The regiment left Warrenton on June 12. It participated in all the cavalry fights from Aldie to Ashby's Gap including Middleburg and Upperville. In the skirmish at Aldie Company F lost Sergeant William Berry. On June 29 the regiment crossed the Potomac River into Maryland at Edwards Ferry and rode towards Frederick City where they skirmished with a body of Confederate cavalry. From Frederick Gregg's Division moved through Westminster, Manchester, and Hanover, Pennsylvania, before reaching Gettysburg.[19]

The Second Division arrived on the Union right flank at about 11:00 a.m. After a few hours rest McIntosh's Brigade was ordered to move down the Hanover Road and relieve the Union infantry that had been skirmishing with the Stonewall Brigade along Brinkerhoff's Ridge. The brigade was involved in heavy skirmishing until 10:00 p.m. when it was ordered to withdraw and camp near the Reserve Artillery Train on the Baltimore Pike.[20]

In conjunction with his infantry attack on the Union center, General Lee ordered Stuart to take his cavalry on a sweep around the Union right flank and attack Meade's wagon parks on July 3. This would not only disrupt communication in the rear, it would hopefully divert reinforcements away from the point of attack for what became known as Pickett's Charge. Stuart occupied Cress' Ridge three miles east of Gettysburg. From this point he could cover the Confederate left and at the same time be in position to attack the Union rear. Covering the Union right was Gregg's Division supported by newly promoted Brigadier General George A. Custer and four regiments of Michigan cavalry.

The Union cavalry intercepted White's Virginia Battalion moving on the Hanover Road. Stuart countered by dismounting a portion of Jenkins' Brigade and sending it forward. Armed with Enfield muskets Jenkins' men could out range the short barreled Union carbines. Before the Confederate attack could gain momentum, Gregg ordered the Third Pennsylvania and First Maryland, supported by guns from the First New Jersey Artillery, to block their advance. As pressure built up Gregg extended his line to the left with additional units. When Stuart's attack stalled for a second time he ordered the brigades of Fitzhugh Lee and Wade Hampton to make a saber charge and cut their way through the Union line. The initial shock of their charge had the desired effect and the blue troopers were forced to retreat. Gregg ordered Custer to counter attack with his "Wolverines" and supported him with both brigades of the Second Division. The Confederate advance was stopped and then pushed back to Cress' Ridge. During the height of the action Colonel Deems was ordered to take the First Maryland and cover the extreme right flank of the Union line. Losses for the two-day battle were two officers and eight enlisted men wounded and one man missing.[21]

A tie at Brandy Station, the Cavalry Corps of the Army of the Potomac could claim its first clear-cut victory in a major engagement at Gettysburg. From that day onward, superior manpower, horseflesh, and repeating rifles, would put the Union Cavalry on the path to victory and the Confederate Cavalry on the road to Appomattox.

Still lethal, Stuart's cavalry covered Lee's retreat back into Virginia. The First Maryland and Gregg's Division joined the Sixth Army Corps in its pursuit. For two weeks after the Battle of Gettysburg dozens of battles and skirmishes were fought to capture wagon trains or force mountain passes. In a skirmish at Emmitsburg, Private Jim Jordon of Company I lost a leg.[22]

General George G. Meade had been given command of the Army of the Potomac just prior to the Battle of Gettysburg. Fortunate to have won the most important battle of the war, he was less successful in attacking Lee before he re-crossed the Potomac River into Virginia. Back in Virginia before the end of July, the First Maryland finished out the summer scouting and skirmishing as before. Losses from several skirmishes in October were 4 enlisted men wounded and 14 missing. In mid-October the regiment was ordered to report to Brigadier General Marsena R. Patrick, Provost Marshal of the Army of the Potomac. Its winter camp for November and December was Brandy Station.[23]

On November 10, Lieutenant Colonel Deems received his discharge. He had led the regiment through two of the most important cavalry battles of the war—Brandy Station and Gettysburg. He was given the rank of Brevet-Colonel and Brevet-Brigadier General for his service during the war. Major Charles H. Russell assumed command of the regiment. A clergyman before the war, he was sometimes referred to as "The Fighting Parson." In December Company M joined the regiment at Brandy Station. Prior to this it had been Captain William H. Orton's Independent Company from Washington, DC.[24]

Although the South suffered significant defeats at Gettysburg and Vicksburg in 1863 the war was far from over. Throughout 1864 the three-year enlistments of many experienced units would reach their completion date. Their efficiency could never be replaced on the battlefield by draftees, substitutes, and the trickle of true volunteers that was the natural byproduct of a protracted war. To remedy this situation the Federal Government offered any solder who had served a minimum of two years a bonus called a bounty and a 30-day leave of absence if he would reenlist for three years or the conclusion

Lt. Col. James M. Deems: Enlisted as a major in 1861. Promoted to lieutenant colonel on October 9, 1862. He led the First Maryland Regiment at Brandy Station and Gettysburg. Deems was discharged in November of 1863. He received the rank of Brevet Brigadier General on March 13, 1865. (D.C.T.)

of the war. The soldiers could reenlist as individuals or, if a large enough number of men in a unit agreed to the proposition, their battery or regiment would have the word "Veteran" added to its title. This would ensure that the best units in the army would not melt away at the height of the next campaign season when victory might well be at hand.

In December of 1863 three-fourths of Company M reenlisted at Brandy Station, as did a total of 169 men throughout the regiment. These men were granted their furloughs in January while the army was in its winter quarters. The balance of the regiment consisting of new recruits and those that had not reenlisted was transferred to Baltimore City and stationed at Camp Lockwood where it was joined by the Veterans at the end of their leave.[25]

The First Maryland Veteran Volunteer Cavalry was assigned to General Henry H. Lockwood's Third Separate Brigade. Andrew W. Evans now commanded the regiment. A West Point graduate and captain in the Sixth U.S. Cavalry, he was commissioned a colonel on December 1, 1863. He would stay with the Marylanders until the end of the war. In April the First Maryland moved to Camp Carroll where it received orders that every cavalry regiment dreaded. It was to proceed to Washington City where it would be dismounted and converted into infantry. Four companies of the First Battalion were still mounted and operating along the railroad between Monocacy Junction and Relay. These were ordered to march to Washington and turn in their horses. The balance of the regiment boarded a train at Camp Carroll on June 5 and arrived at Washington the same day.[26]

During the next few days the men turned in their cavalry equipment and then marched across Long Bridge to Fort Albany where they drew their infantry weapons and ammunition. On June 10 the regiment embarked on the U.S. steamer *Guide* and arrived two days later at Bermuda Hundred in Virginia. Here it suffered the further indignation of being assigned to General Kautz cavalry division as infantry. The strength of the regiment at this time was 646 officers and men.[27]

The First Maryland was now part of the Department of Virginia and North Carolina commanded by Major General Benjamin F. Butler. It was soon assigned to General Alfred Terry's First Division of the Tenth Army Corps and reported to General R. S. Foster's Third Brigade at Deep Bottom on June 24.[28]

In August the regiment saw its first action as infantry. On the fourteenth of the month the men marched out of its camp at Deep Bottom with four days cooked rations in their haversacks. It had proceeded less than two miles when it became engaged with the enemy. When the brigade charged, the First Maryland carried a line of rifle-pits and captured two Rebel officers and 1 enlisted man. The regiment lost 2 officers and 19 enlisted men wounded and 2 enlisted men killed. That night the brigade camped at Strawberry Plains. On the fifteenth the regiment took up a position behind the Second Corps skirmish line. Despite the fact that the regiment remained inactive all day nearly 30 men were felled by sunstroke due to the intense heat. The next morning the regiment was in an action along the Charles City Road. In a charge with the One Hundred and Fifth Pennsylvania Infantry it captured one line of enemy works and temporarily occupied a second. Losses on this day were 3 officers and 63 enlisted men wounded. Fourteen enlisted men were killed and 19 were missing. The regiment lost 3 more men before returning to camp at Deep Bottom on August 21.[29]

A few days later the First Maryland marched to Petersburg where it was assigned a position in the trenches in front of Fort Hell. Twenty men and one officer from Company A were assigned to duty at Tenth Corps headquarters. The balance of the regiment was under constant fire day and night. On September 3 about 20 men from Company I were discharged having completed their enlistment. While waiting in line to be mustered out, one man had the misfortune of being hit by a musket ball that broke his hip.[30]

While the regiment was participating in the siege of Petersburg, Brigadier General August V. Kautz wrote to the Army of the James Headquarters complaining that his Cavalry Division had been greatly reduced through details and transfers. He requested that the First Maryland be remounted and assigned to his command. In modern parlance, his request was put on the fast track. Three days later General Butler wrote back, "Approved." On September 21 Butler wrote directly to General Grant requesting the horses be released from the Cavalry Bureau. On the 27th the regiment was ordered to report to Bermuda Hundred "...at once for the purpose of being mounted and equipped." Glorious news for the First Maryland until they were ordered back to Petersburg as infantry the very next day! The horses and equipment were not yet available. Finally, on October 3, the regiment was officially transferred to the Cavalry Division. Colonel Evans was given command of the Third Brigade, which consisted of his regiment and the First Mounted Rifles New York Volunteers. Lieutenant Colonel Jacob H. Counselman assumed command of the First Maryland.[31]

The regiment's first action as remounted cavalry came on the Darbytown Road on October 13. Company C lost 2 men killed, 3 wounded and 5 missing. In Company E Private John Geyer was shot below the right eye and Andrew Hindrey in his right thigh. Private Henry Hoffer was struck in the right arm by a shell fragment. The regiment also participated in the attack on the enemy's works on the Charles City and Williamsburg Road on October 27. After these engagements the regiment went into camp near the New Market Road and stayed there throughout the winter of 1864.[32] In the spring of 1864 Ulysses S. Grant was rewarded for his victories in the West with a promotion to General in Chief of the Army. Grant came east and made his headquarters with the Army of the Potomac. He brought with him General Phillip H. Sheridan to command the Cavalry Corps of the Army of the Potomac. Sheridan reorganized the Union cavalry into three divisions. The First Maryland joined his command on April 1, part of General Ronald S. Mackenzie's brigade, and engaged the enemy at Five Forks. Two days later one battalion was assigned to Major General Sheridan's headquarters. When the Confederate lines were broken around Richmond in April of 1865, Grant sent Sheridan to bring the wounded Army of Northern Virginia to bay. After capturing a fourth of Lee's army at Saylor's Creek, Sheridan sped past the fleeing Rebel army and cut the Richmond and Danville Railroad on April 5 forcing Lee to surrender at Appomattox Court House on April 9. The First Maryland Veteran Volunteer Cavalry Regiment was there and in itself represented a history of Cavalry Corps in the East.

After the surrender of Lee's Army the regiment, with Mackenzie's Brigade, was assigned to the Department of Virginia commanded by Major General E.O.C. Ord. Usually camped at Manchester, Virginia, the First Maryland operated between Richmond and Ashland doing provost duty and escorting refugees to their homes. The regiment was mustered out of Federal service on August 8, 1865. It had participated in 60 battles and skirmishes between January 1, 1862, and April 9, 1864. Its battle deaths and other losses numbered 201 officers and men.[33]

Corporal William Shaffer: Enlisted in Company B, Second Maryland Cavalry on
June 24, 1863. Mustered out January 26, 1864. (D.C.T.)

SECOND MARYLAND CAVALRY REGIMENT

After the First Battle of Bull Run was fought the standard term of enlistment became three years or the end of the war. Exceptions to this rule came during the summer months of both 1863 and 1864, when a Confederate invasion of the North caused emergency units to be called up for periods of three to six months. This was the case with the Second Maryland Cavalry. It was organized in June of 1863 as Lee's Army of Northern Virginia pushed its way across the Potomac River en route to the Pennsylvania town of Gettysburg. Its term of enlistment was six months.

In reality the Second Regiment was only a battalion of five companies. Companies A, B, and E were recruited in Baltimore City. The men of Company C came from both Howard County and Baltimore City. Company D was organized in Washington, D.C. No field or staff grade officers were ever mustered into its service. Command of the Second Maryland went to its senior Captain, the 44-year-old William F. Bragg.[1]

After the five companies were consolidated in Baltimore City, they were sent to Annapolis and placed under the command of Colonel Carlos A. Waite. During their six month tour of duty, the companies were detached throughout Anne Arundel and Calvert counties and did provost duty in Maryland's capital city.[2]

One of the privates in Company A was Edward H. McKeldin, the grandfather of a future governor of the state, Theodore R. McKeldin. Edward McKeldin first enlisted in 1861, in Company B of the Baltimore Light Infantry, but was never mustered into Federal service. In 1863 the 39-year-old McKeldin decided to try it again and enlisted in the Second Cavalry. His company was assigned to provost marshal duty in Annapolis. On July 5, 1863, he wrote a letter to his wife Sophia in Baltimore. In it he described the company's situation at Camp Parole. "…43 of us guarding 3,600 men…" which he called "hard cases." He also requested she get a box and send him among other things a razor and soap brush, a pint of good whiskey, tobacco, and some clothing.[3]

Captain Bragg commanded the five companies of the Second Maryland for their entire term of enlistment other than a few days in October when he was under arrest. He was charged by Colonel Waite with trading a "…Bay Mare Colt, which had been seized and taken for the military service…" for a watch and money from a Lieutenant Grinnell. He was also charged with trading a "…Grey Horse Colt, which had been seized…" to Mr. Alfred Browning for another horse and money. The case was dropped and Bragg returned to duty.[4]

While on active duty 13 men died of disease. Several of these were buried in the National Cemetery on West Street in Annapolis. Others were buried the following year. Here are their names and the information on their markers:

Britton, James, Pvt. Co. E, December 21, 1864, D1274
Fuget, George, Cpl. Co. D, November 18, 1863, F2155
Jarbo, William, Pvt. Co. D, November 22, 1863, F2156
Kelley, Ervine, Pvt. Co. D, September 20, 1864, E1727
Lutman, Henry, Pvt. Co. F, March 24, 1864, K1001
Macomb, Henry J. Pvt. Co. C, August 30, 1863, F2015[5]

Others departed in a less permanent fashion. Private William H. Stone of Company B deserted on October 17, 1863. At the time he owed the Federal government 92 cents for camp and garrison equipment. To this lofty sum was added $32.00 for clothing, 48 cents for a haversack, and 44 cents for a canteen.[6]

At the end of their enlistment in January of 1864, 70 men of the Second Maryland re-enlisted for three years in the Third Maryland Cavalry Regiment. A lesser number joined Cole's Cavalry. Companies A and B were mustered out at Camp Lockwood in Baltimore on January 26, 1864. Company E left the service on January 31. Companies C and D were discharged on February 6, 1864.[7]

Private William H. Stone: Second Maryland Cavalry. (D.C.T.)

THIRD MARYLAND CAVALRY REGIMENT

(THE BRADFORD DRAGOONS)

O f all the companies, batteries, and regiments raised by the state of Maryland during the Civil War, none can compare with the composition and leadership of the Third Cavalry Regiment. Named for Maryland's second wartime governor, its commanding officer was a West Point graduate and soldier of fortune. As for the enlisted men, nearly half of them came from Rebel prisoners held at Fort Delaware. Once the regiment was organized, it was shipped off to Louisiana where its companies were dispersed among the bayous of that region.

Authorization to raise a three-year regiment was issued by the Federal government in August of 1863. Its first commanding officer was Charles Carroll

Tavis. Tavis was born in Philadelphia. He graduated from West Point in the class of 1845 and served in the armies of Egypt, France, and Turkey, as well as that of the United States. He was a Lieutenant Colonel in the Fourth Delaware Infantry when given temporary command of the Third Maryland and transferred with his existing rank.

While the regiment was being formed in Baltimore City, Tavis was ordered to Fort Delaware to recruit men for his regiment from among the Rebel POW's being held there. A Confederate prisoner could trade short rations and the uncertainty of captivity for his freedom by signing the "Oath of Allegiance" and enlisting in the Union Army for three years. This was not the only time in history an army recruited from among its enemies. During World War II the German Army sought volunteers from among its Central European prisoners for use in labor details in France.[1]

During the Civil War Confederate volunteers serving in the Union Army were called "Galvanized Yankees." Most of these men were sent to the Western Territories where they fought Indians and guarded wagon trains. This served the dual purpose of freeing able-bodied men for combat "Back East" and separated the ex-Rebels from their homeland where the inclination to desert would be much stronger. Therefore, it was very unusual when the volunteers from Fort Delaware were sent to a regiment that was destined for service in the Southern States. Their numbers were credited to Maryland's enlistment quota and the soldiers received the Federal bounty money being offered at that time.[2]

Tavis' recruiting mission was highly successful. On September 8, 1863, Special Order #236 transferred 120 men from Fort Delaware to the Third Maryland. Three days later Special Order #248 released an additional 280 Rebel recruits to the regiment. These two groups became companies D, E, F, and G. They joined companies A, B, C, H, and I that had been recruited in Baltimore City. Company K was composed of men who had re-enlisted after serving in the Second Maryland Cavalry.[3]

The regiment was stationed at Camp Schenck while it completed its organization. In October it received 800 horses. Total strength at this time was 602 officers and men. In December the Third Maryland was assigned to the Cavalry Reserve of the Eighth Army Corps. Tavis was given command of the Reserve, which contained elements of the First Connecticut, First Delaware,

Colonel Charles Carroll Tavis: A graduate of the United States Military Academy class of 1845, Tavis served in the armies of Egypt, France, Turkey, and the United States. As first commander of the Third Maryland Cavalry Regiment, he was highly successful recruiting "Galvanized Yankees" from among the Rebel prisoners at Fort Delaware. (D.C.T.)

and the Third Maryland temporarily under the command of Major William Kesley.[4]

During this period of time Tavis set a pattern of behavior that would last throughout his association with the regiment. On November 6, he reported himself under arrest to Lieutenant Colonel Cheseborough and requested "… what charges are preferred against me and by whom…" Tavis had conspired to aid John Frazier, Jr., the Provost Marshal of Kent County, in winning a clerk's position in the local court. After arresting everyone thought to be voting against Frazier, he took over the office of *The Kent News* in Chestertown and ordered circulars printed that were, in fact, instructions to the local populous on how to vote in the upcoming state election. One of these documents found their way to General Schenk's headquarters and, dubbed "Colonel Tavis' Last Order," led to his arrest.[5]

On November 25, Colonel Tavis wrote a letter to Major General Schenck reminding him of his promise to recommend Tavis to the Governor of Maryland for promotion to full colonel and permanent command of the Third Cavalry, a game move for a man under arrest. This was followed up on January 3, 1864, with a request for ten days sick leave supported by a medical certificate from John M. Stevenson, the regimental surgeon. It stated that Tavis was "…suffering from nervous prostration…" and "…great mental anxiety produced by the turn of affairs relative to this officers receiving his commission."[6]

Governor Bradford was not giving in, and Tavis was not giving up. On the very next day Henry Winter Davis, a member of the House of Representatives from Maryland, wrote Secretary of War Edward M. Stanton requesting his intervention in the promotion of Tavis to a full colonel. Four days later Congressman Davis received a reply. "…your friend C. C. Tavis has been commissioned as Colonel of the 3rd Maryland Cavalry."[7]

In December the Third Maryland was transferred to Major General Nathaniel P. Banks' Department of the Gulf. The first contingent to leave consisted of companies A, B, C, H, and I under the command of Major Byron Kirby. The regimental staff and Company F followed in the steamer *Charles Thomas.* By February all the companies had arrived in Louisiana. After processing through the Cavalry Depot in New Orleans, the regiment was transferred to Madisonville, Louisiana.[8]

During its first two months in the Department of the Gulf, the regiment was dispersed over a wide area and usually participated in company size operations. On January 26, Company G arrived at Madisonville aboard the steamer *N. P. Banks.* First Lieutenant Francis R. Haight took 21 men and joined companies B and C on a scout to Henning's Farm. The patrol returned with four prisoners and several horses. On February 11, Company C had a skirmish 20 miles from their base camp at Madisonville. Corporal John C. Klinke and Private Wilhelm Engel were reported captured. On the same day companies E and H went to Covington, Mandeville, and Lewisburg. They returned with three prisoners. In mid-February Colonel Tavis made a rare personal appearance in the field and led Company H on a scout that netted four prisoners. The largest operation at this time consisted of six companies led by Captain Eli D. Grinder to Ponchatoula. Company I made six scouts in January and five in February, covering a total of 438 miles. Colonel Tavis also took the field in early March when he led three companies of his regiment on reconnaissance to Madisonville. The purpose of the expedition was to clear the area of guerrillas commanded by a man named Greenley. No contact with the enemy was made until the Union force reached the fords on the Chappapela River which were defended by elements of the Ninth and Tenth battalions of Louisiana cavalry. The Marylanders charged the fords and captured 10 of the enemy with their horses and equipment. They also captured a number of bloodhounds used to track down conscripts and freed 30 Negroes captured near Fort Pike.[9]

In the spring of 1864 President Lincoln approved an expedition against Shreveport which was both the headquarters of Lieutenant General E. Kirby Smith and the Confederate capital of Louisiana. General Banks marched his army overland to link up with a combined infantry and naval force under the command of Admiral David D. Porter that was moving up the Red River. In the consolidation that took place prior to the campaign, the Third Maryland was ordered to report to Brashear City where it joined Brigadier General C. Grover's Second Division of the Nineteenth Army Corps. The advance up the Red River was greatly impeded by the rapids above Alexandria, causing the city to become a base camp for the Red River Expedition. The Third Maryland was assigned to guard the supply depot at Alexandria and did not participate in the advance upriver. Banks Army was defeated at Mansfield on April 8. Porter lost several vessels during his return trip down the Red River which was plagued by shallow water and Confederate artillery.[10]

A report was issued on May 25 concerning the strength of the Cavalry Division listed the Third Maryland Regiment with ten companies totaling 645

Sergeant Edward S. Harding, alias John L. Harding: Enlisted in 1861 as a private in Company D of the First Potomac Home Brigade Infantry Regiment. A severe illness caused him to be discharged on May 5, 1862. To avoid connection with his previous medical condition, Harding re-enlisted in the Third Maryland Cavalry Regiment under the name of John L. Harding on September 7, 1864 at his hometown of Frederick, Maryland. A private in Company I, he was promoted to saddler sergeant and transferred to the regimental staff. Harding was mustered out with the rest of the regiment at Vicksburg, Mississippi, on September 7, 1865. In 1921 he suffered a stroke. Contained in the General Affidavit submitted for government assistance was the statement, "We have no sons that are in the World War." (Photograph and biographical information courtesy of Mr. & Mrs. Walter R. Harding, Jr.)

men. One company was on detached duty at Thibodeaux and another assigned to pioneer duty. The latter was probably Company D which reported in October that "...it has been constantly engaged in sawing lumber, ...cutting fire wood, building railroads and wharves, and in general fatigue labors." The regiment was again operating without its commanding officer. On May 28 Colonel Tavis wrote two letters to Major George B. Drake, A.A.G. Department of the Gulf from the Saint Charles Hotel in New Orleans. In the first he requested the limits of his arrest be extended to allow exercise on account of his failed health after 58 days of confinement. In the second he requested a Court Marshal to review his case—having been suspended from command since the first of April.[11]

On June 4, 1864, his wish was granted and a review board established for his Court Marshal. He was charged with "Conduct to the prejudice of Good Order and Military Discipline" for organizing a public race between two government horses and allowing other officers to place bets. For this he was found guilty. A second charge of "Conduct unbecoming an Officer and a Gentleman," was charged for allowing enlisted men to bet on the same race. To this he was found not guilty.[12]

As soon as the trial was over Tavis issued charges against Lieutenant Colonel Byron, who was then in charge of the regiment, "...for drunkenness, incapacity and violation of the 25th Article of War...." When Byron was released from the charges without a trial, Tavis submitted his resignation. It was a gamble that did not pay off. Major General J. J. Reynolds, commanding the Defenses of New Orleans, reviewed the request with the following endorsement, "...since he (Tavis) has been in the department he has been inefficient and insubordinate and as an officer and I recommend that he be discharged for the good of the service."

Tavis was not one to go with a whimper. He wrote a three-page letter to Major General Canby bestowing his own virtues and deriding Lieutenant Colonel Kirby. "My own record as a soldier in Europe and America is clean and honorable..." As for Lieutenant Colonel Kirby, he claimed his once fine regiment was "...the most demoralized if not the very worst in the Army of the United States..." He could not understand why his resignation had been accepted and threatened to take the whole matter to the President. Charles Carroll Tavis had his revenge. Discharged on July 30, 1864, "For the good of the service," he was given the rank of Brevet Brigadier General in March of 1865 "For gallant and meritorious services during the war." Tavis died in Paris, France, in 1900 and is buried in that city's Montparnasse Cemetery.[13]

While Tavis was camped out at the Saint Charles for a total of 107 days, his regiment was in the field. Companies B and C were stationed at Morganza. In May Company B had 2 men wounded and 4 horses killed in a skirmish. Company H was at Alexandria. It spent every day during the month of April in the saddle, covering 347 miles and fighting one skirmish. In May it moved to Napoleonville. En route from Alexandria to Morganza, Company G fought skirmishes on May 17 and 18. One man and three horses were killed. Company K had a more profitable time. On a scout from Thibodeaux to the Bay of Natchez, it captured three prisoners and $3,000 in United States treasury notes on May 23. In June the company was transferred to Donaldsonville. While scouting in the direction of Bayou Goula it captured a Confederate paymaster with $50,000 in Confederate money and $8,000 worth of contraband goods.[14]

The controversy between its commanders must have taken its toll on the regiment. On June 17, 1864, General William H. Emery, commander of the Nineteenth Army Corps, wrote to General Canby's headquarters. "Colonel Davis reports 400 recruits just arrived... These as well as the Third Maryland Cavalry can be of no use to use on campaign, but on the contrary will be an embarrassment." A week later the regiment was relieved from duty with the Cavalry Division and transferred to the Defenses of New Orleans. On July 7, in accordance with Special Order Number 179, the Third Maryland was ordered to turn in its horses and cavalry equipment and draw infantry weapons and accouterments. Its effective strength at the time was 320.[15]

Now an infantry regiment, the Third Maryland Cavalry (Dismounted), was assigned to General Gordon Granger's Third Brigade in the Third Division of the Nineteenth Army Corps. Elements of the regiment took part in the operations against Fort Morgan and Fort Gains during the summer of 1864. In October six companies were inspected at Fort Gains on Dauphin Island, Alabama. First Lieutenant C. S. Sargent reported to General Granger, commanding the District of West Florida and Southern Alabama, that the Third Maryland was, "...in the worst condition of the troops in South Alabama. Besides being in bad condition as to its general appearance and drill

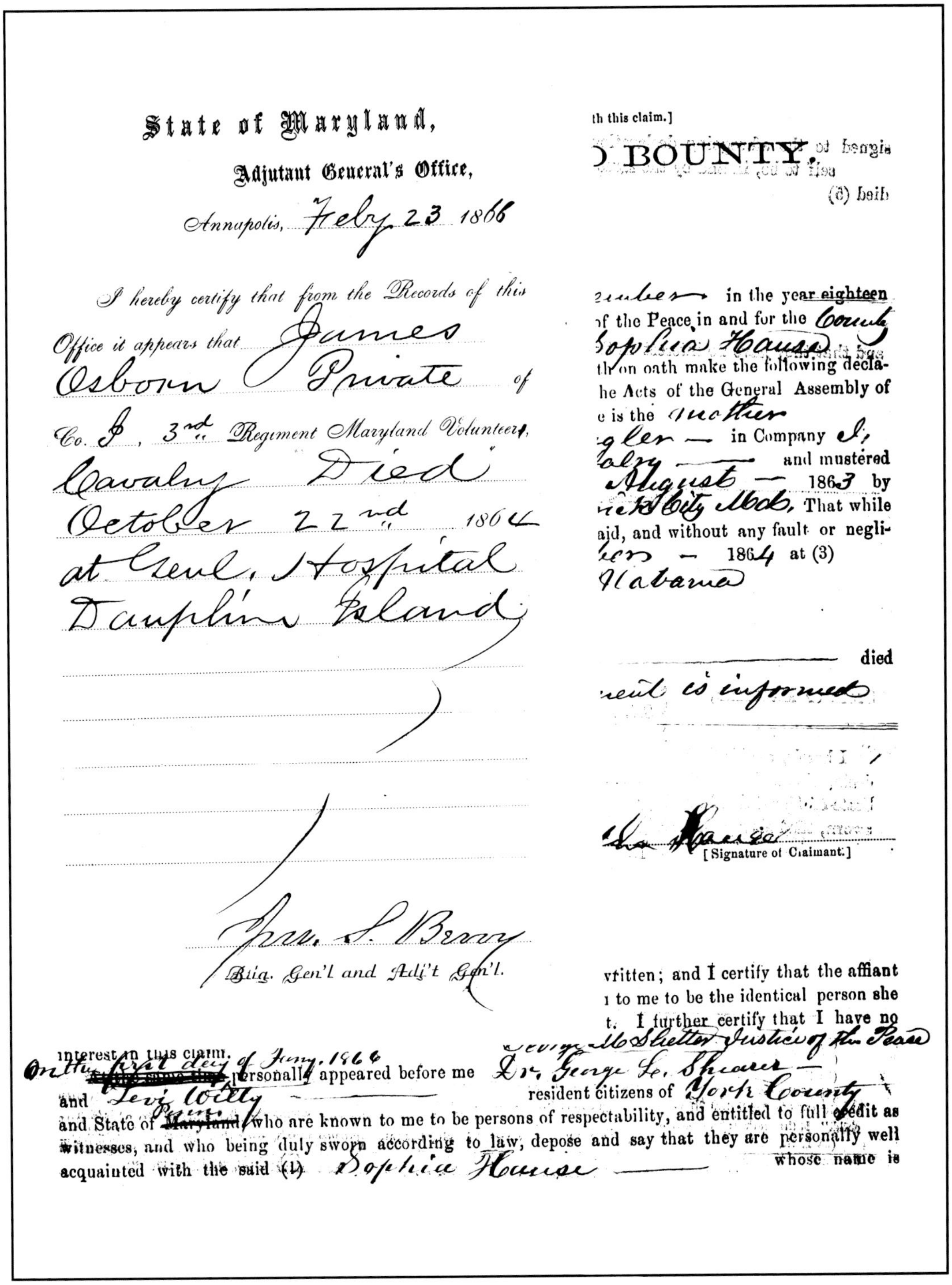

State of Maryland,

Adjutant General's Office,

Annapolis, Feby 23 1866

I hereby certify that from the Records of this Office it appears that James Osborn Private of Co. I, 3rd Regiment Maryland Volunteers, Cavalry Died October 22nd 1864 at Genl. Hospital Dauphin Island

Jno. S. Berry
Brig. Gen'l and Adj't Gen'l.

th this claim.]

) BOUNTY.

(3) beih

...ember in the year eighteen ...f the Peace in and for the County ... Sophia Hause ... th on oath make the following decla... he Acts of the General Assembly of ... e is the mother ... gler — in Company I, ...alry — and mustered ... August — 1863 by ...ck City Md. That while ...aid, and without any fault or negli... ...ber — 1864 at (3) ... Alabama

died

...ent is informed

... Hause
[Signature of Claimant.]

...written; and I certify that the affiant ... to me to be the identical person she ...t. I further certify that I have no interest in this claim. George McSletter Justice of the Peace

On the first day of Jany. 1866 personally appeared before me Dr. George L. Shearer and Levi Witty resident citizens of York County and State of Penna. who are known to me to be persons of respectability, and entitled to full credit as witnesses, and who being duly sworn according to law, depose and say that they are personally well acquainted with the said (1) Sophia Hause — whose name is

Bounty Document: Private James Osborn enlisted in Company I of the Third Maryland Cavalry on August 17, 1863. He served as a bugler. Osborn died in the General Hospital at Dauphin Island, Alabama, on October 22, 1864, of typhoid fever. His mother, Sophia Kause, presented this notarized document to the State of Maryland as a claim for her deceased son's unpaid enlistment bounty of $300.00. After the war a virtual industry was created for the representation of claims to the state and federal governments for bounty and pension money. (D.C.T.)

and general duties, the 3rd Md Cavalry is reported lax in discipline and having inefficient and dirty quarters and camp."[16]

By the end of 1864 the losses from combat, sickness, and desertion took its toll on the regiment. During the Civil War units were expected to draw replacements from their home base. This was not possible for the Third Cavalry, which was serving farther from home than any other white unit from Maryland in either army. Their only alternative was to consolidate companies in order to maintain combat efficiency. This was done during the month of December. The men of Company A were transferred to Company B. Company C went to Company I; Company D to Company E; Company G to Company F; and Company H to Company K. Byron Kirby continued to command the now battalion size regiment.[17]

Reports from February 1865 show all six companies as part of the garrison at Fort Gains. Its effective strength was down to 327 officers and enlisted men. At the end of April all detachments were ordered to reunite with the regiment at Fort Gains and board steamers for New Orleans. Arriving there on May 6, the regiment marched to Greenville where the men turned in their infantry weapons and were issued cavalry equipment. Literally back in the saddle again, the Third Maryland was ordered to Natchez, Mississippi, where it relieved the First Texas Cavalry US.[18]

From Natchez the regiment was ordered to Vicksburg to be mustered out on September 7, 1865. Those who had survived the swamps, enemy, and Colonel Tavis' leadership, were sent back to Baltimore for their final pay and honorable discharges. They had served in the backwaters of the war. For them there would be no "Brandy Station" or Yellow Tavern" battle honors painted on their regimental colors, but they were veterans just the same.[19]

COMPANY A PURNELL LEGION CAVALRY

As detailed in the chapter on the artillery, the Purnell Legion was a combined arms unit consisting of infantry, artillery, and cavalry. At no time during the war did the Legion function as a whole or the cavalry as a battalion. Therefore, the history of each of the three companies will be given separately.

Company A was organized at Pikesville between September and November of 1861. Its commanding officer was Captain Robert E. Duvall. Captain Duvall enlisted on September 15 at the age of 49. The Company Muster Roll contains the notation that he supplied his own horse and equipment. Company A was assigned to Major General John A. Dix's command as part of the Middle Department. This department encompassed parts of Delaware, the Eastern Shore counties of Maryland and Virginia, and the area west of Baltimore City as far as the Monocacy River. Troops assigned to this department were collectively referred to as the Eighth Army Corps. Brigadier General Henry H. Lockwood commanded all the troops stationed on the Eastern Shore. Company A remained at Pikesville until the end of the year.[1]

On January 14, 1862, General Dix advised General Lockwood that Company A would soon be sent to his command and requested that shelter for both the men and horses be prepared. Surprisingly, up to this time Duvall's men had not been issued arms, but General Dix was confident that revolvers could be procured before their departure.[2]

Company A spent March and April at Franktown, Virginia, looking for blockade-runners and recruiters for the Confederate Army. In May it moved to Eastville in Northhampton County where it remained throughout the summer, before ending the year of 1862 at Drummondtown in Accomac County, Virginia.[3]

In 1863 Company A moved back in to Maryland, spending March and April in Saint Mary's County. By June they had moved to Annapolis Junction. This was the point where the Annapolis and Elk Ridge Railroad met the Washington Branch of the Baltimore and Ohio. It was through this point that General Benjamin F. Butler had moved troops from Annapolis to "Save the Capitol" in 1861. June of 1863 was also a time of great excitement. The yet unnamed Gettysburg Campaign was getting under way as Lee's army moved down the Shenandoah Valley and into Maryland. Captain Duvall was ordered to take his 73 men west to Monocacy Bridge and scout the area for the infantry guarding the railroad there.[4]

On June 28, Company A left Monocacy Bridge at daybreak with orders to escort two guns of Rank's Pennsylvania Battery to Relay where they were to be used in defense of the Thomas Viaduct and other railroad property. The two units moved east along the National Pike and camped near Cooksville in Howard County. That night their pickets were driven in by the advance of J.E.B. Stuart's cavalry division and the famous captured wagon train. Duvall sent Sergeant Andrew Duncan and Private Jonathan Norris back to Frederick to warn the Federal commander there of Stuart presence. In a hasty retreat under the cover of darkness he lost some camp equipment and four horses but managed to save his men and Rank's guns. Near Popular Springs Duvall was fortunate to fall in with Colonel John B. McIntosh's First Brigade of the Second Cavalry Division, Army of the Potomac. He stayed with this command until the end of the Gettysburg Campaign. When the two guns and Duvall's company did not reach Relay as expected, General Schenck, then commanding the Middle Department, reported them captured to General Halleck. It was two days before their true status was known.[5]

Gregg's Cavalry Division covered the right flank of the Union Army as it

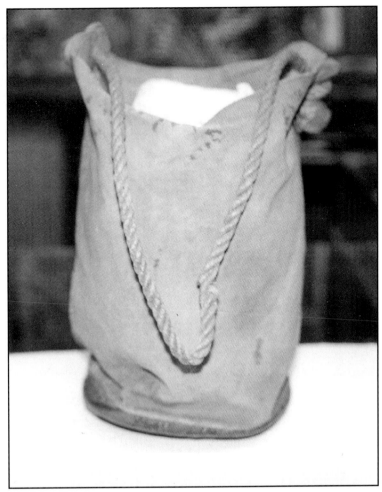

Feed Bag: A standard item for every trooper, Private William F. Channell used this one to feed his mount. Channell served as a bugler in Company A of the Purnell Legion Cavalry from February of 1864 to July of 1865. (Union Room Collection, MNGMHS)

moved north. Macintosh's Brigade marched throughout the night of June 29 and entered Westminster at daybreak where they skirmished with the rear guard of Stuart's cavalry. The brigade then moved on to Manchester where it camped for the night. Moving again at dawn on July 1, Gregg's Division reached Hanover, Pennsylvania, at 1 a.m. After only two hours rest the column set out for Gettysburg which it reached about 11 a.m. on July 2.

After a few hours rest Gregg was ordered to replace a regiment of infantry from the Eleventh Corps skirmishing with Confederate infantry on Brinkerhoff's Ridge. He ordered McIntosh's brigade to move down the

Hanover Road and engage the enemy. At this time McIntosh's brigade consisted of five regiments including the First Maryland Cavalry, the recently acquired Company A of the Purnell Legion, and the two pieces of artillery from Rank's Battery.

Ranks guns were unlimbered in the middle of the road and 50 men were sent forward to test the enemy's line. They were repulsed by a regiment of Rebel infantry. When a large group of enemy soldiers were spotted on top of Brinkerhoff's Ridge, Rank's guns sent two rounds in their direction and drove them to cover. Around 6 p.m. the Third Pennsylvania Regiment advanced at a trot in the direction of Gettysburg. Two of its squadrons dismounted and were deployed as skirmishers on the side of the hill. The men of the Purnell Legion company were also ordered to dismount and formed on the left of the Pennsylvanians.

A stone wall ran across the top of Brinkerhoff's Ridge. Both sides immediately perceived the importance of its shelter and charged for the wall. Fire from Rank's guns slowed the pace of the Second Virginia Infantry enough for the Union cavalrymen to reach their objective first and deliver a withering volley of carbine fire at the range of only 20 feet. The Confederates then fell back to a sheltered position and continued to exchange fire until after sundown. At 10 p.m. McIntosh's Brigade was withdrawn from the line and ordered to camp for the night near the Reserve Artillery Train on the Baltimore Pike.[6]

On July 3, General Lee ordered Stuart to take his cavalry on a sweep around the Union right flank and strike the rear of General Meade's line while Picket drove home the infantry attack from the front. Patrolling the Union right flank was Gregg's division and Custer's Brigade of Michigan cavalry. Gregg placed his two brigades between the Baltimore Pike and the Hanover Road. He sent out the First New Jersey on foot toward Cress' Ridge. They struck dismounted cavalry from Jenkin's Brigade behind a fence line on the Rummel farm and became fully engaged. Two squadrons of the Third Pennsylvania Regiment and Company A of the Purnell Legion were sent forward and extended the Union line to the left. Gregg was determined to disrupt the Confederate advance before it could gain momentum. His Horse Artillery shelled the Rebel sharpshooters out of the Rummel barn and disabled two of Stuart's guns. After extending his line to the left of Company A with four squadrons from the Sixth Michigan, Gregg ordered a charge that was at first successful. Stuart then counter attacked with the brigades of Fitzhugh Lee and Wade Hampton, which sent Company A and the rest of the Union line rearward. The East Cavalry Battle reached its climax when Custer threw his Michigan Brigade against the onrushing Confederates. Supported by both brigades of Gregg's division they stopped and then pushed the Rebel cavalry back to Cress' Ridge. Company A fell in with its adopted brigade and helped with the counterattack. It suffered no casualties in its two days of fighting at Gettysburg.[7]

Company A remained with the Army of the Potomac as it followed Lee's retreat back into Virginia. It was then transferred to the nearly all Maryland brigade commanded by Colonel William P. Maulsby in Maryland Heights. The brigade was part of the defense force at Harper's Ferry commanded by General Lockwood who had been transferred from the Eastern Shore.[8]

By the end of the year Company A was stationed at Eastville, which was now part of the Department of Virginia and North Carolina under the command of General Butler and the Army of the James.[9]

In January of 1864 Sergeant Thomas R. Herbert transferred to the Second U.S.C.T. Cavalry with the rank of Captain. Sergeant James C. Foy went also with a promotion to First Lieutenant.[10]

At dawn on the morning of March 5, 1864, Captain Fitzhugh led a raiding party of 40 to 50 men against Cherrystone, Virginia. Corporal Charles E. Osmond was in charge of an eight-man detachment on guard there. He and five of his men were captured as well as all eight horses. The other two men were guarding the telegraph line a mile and a half away and escaped capture. The Rebels also captured two ships lying at the wharf. The steamer *Iolas* was bonded and the government steam tug *Titan* was taken as a prize and used for transportation back to the western shore of Virginia. Before leaving the Rebels destroyed the telegraph office, guard house and $2.000 worth of commissary stores. Unable to remove the horses, Fitzhugh ordered them shot. Captain Duvall arrived with a relief force just as the tug was pulling away and was unable to save his men.[11]

Company A remained on duty at Eastville throughout the summer and fall of 1864. In October Captain Duvall was suffering with a fever and was not able to command his company. There being no Post Surgeon at Eastville, the Provost Marshal, Major Frank C. White, requested a 30-day leave of absence

Gettysburg Monument: Company A was the only Purnell company to participate in a major cavalry battle. Their monument is located on the East Cavalry Battlefield, site of Stuart's repulse on July 3, 1863. The state of Maryland dedicated the monument on October 23, 1890. After the dedication, the survivors attended their first reunion at the City Hotel in Gettysburg. (Gettysburg Monument Report)

so that Duvall could go home and recuperate. He returned to his company in November. The following month he was ordered to Washington City to "...settle accounts and be mustered out." Unfortunately, during his sick leave in October, First Lieutenant Joseph W. Strong failed to properly account for his absence on the company muster rolls and he was not able to procure his discharge until January of 1865.[12]

Lieutenant Strong assumed command of the 71 enlisted men in Company A when Captain Duvall departed for Washington. Their principle duty was to patrol the telegraph line from Cape Charles to the Maryland line and prevent the locals from communicating with the Western Shore of Virginia. On December 17, the company was scheduled to be transferred to Norfolk and discharged from the service. Major White, now a Lt. Colonel and the Post Commander, delayed their departure until replacements could be found to guard the 40 miles of telegraph line in his department.[13]

A week later Company A was transferred to the Army of the Potomac by Special Order #156, but Lt. Colonel White continued to hold onto them throughout most of January, 1865. On January 23, White received the following instructions:

"Embark the Purnell Legion at once, to
report to Colonel Morrison at Fort Magruder.
By order of Brigadier-General Shepley"

White replied the same day that the company was just being cycled out of his post and would not be consolidated for a day or two. After that they would need a boat to take them to Norfolk as none was at Eastville.[14]

On January 25, General E.O.C. Ord canceled the transfer and Company A remained at Eastville throughout the winter and spring of 1865. Lieutenant Strong was discharged in April of 1865. First Lieutenant Gideon G. Herbert commanded the company until it was mustered out on July 28, 1865.[15]

COMPANY B PURNELL LEGION CAVALRY

After Company B was mustered into Federal service it remained at the Pikesville Arsenal until the end of 1861. Its company grade officers were Captain Thomas H. Watkins, First Lieutenant Henry Clayton, and Second Lieutenant Joseph S. Whittington. Captain Watkins is as excellent example of a well-to-do Marylander who chose defense of the Union over states rights. His life and death contradicts the popular misconception that all Maryland Yankees were either newly arrived immigrants or paid substitutes.

At the outbreak of the war Thomas Watkins lived on his parents' estate "The Locust" in Anne Arundel Count. His father, Doctor Ben Watkins, was a prominent citizen and slaveholder in this very pro-Southern region of the state. Yet, when the war came both father and son supported the Federal government. During the summer of 1861, Watkins assisted Governor Hicks as a civilian in recruiting efforts throughout the state. In December of 1861 he enlisted at Fort McHenry and was given command of Company B.[1]

In January of 1862 both companies A and B of the Purnell Legion moved from Pikesville to the fairgrounds in Baltimore. At the end of February Company A departed for the Eastern Shore. Company A remained until May when it was transferred to Camp Carroll on the west side of Baltimore City.

On October 12, Captain Watkins reported with his company to Annapolis for special duty under the direction of Governor August W. Bradford.[2]

In February of 1863 Company A was ordered to report to Lt. Colonel George Sangster for Provost Marshal duty at Camp Parole. Camp Parole was a large receiving depot for Union soldiers just outside the city of Annapolis. At this point in the war both governments preferred to parole prisoners, that is, have them sign a pledge not to return to active duty rather than hold them in prison. Soldiers who were paroled during the first year of the war were allowed to go home while the paperwork procedure of being "exchanged" for a like number of Rebels was being carried out. Unfortunately, when notified to return to active duty many Union soldiers found home life too inviting and failed to do so. To avoid this problem "Parole Camps" were established to keep the men under military control until they could be exchanged and then escorted back to their units.[3]

A parole camp was little more than a Union prison for Union soldiers. As draftees and bounty jumpers entered the army there was an explosion of crime around Camp Parole and the city of Annapolis. Provost duty was anything but a pleasant assignment. Private William H. Pryce of Company B wrote a letter to his uncle in February of 1863 in which he recorded a snow fall of nearly a foot which resulted in very little trouble from the prisoners as they, "cannot get about." He went on to say that his detail had escorted 200 men to the dock that morning, bound for a reunion with their regiments. To this he added:

> "I don't know what they will do with us when
> they leave here, but I expect we will be sent to
> the field. I had rather be there. Here we are in
> danger of losing our lives among our own men
> and if I am to be killed I rather a Rebel do it."[4]

In May Company B returned to the Defenses of Baltimore under the command of General Erastus B. Tyler. It was detailed for two months to Smyrna, Delaware, returning to Baltimore in September of 1863 only to be detailed to Bryantown in Charles County for the months of November and December.[5]

In January of 1864 Captain Watkins applied for a 15-day leave of absence and married the 18-year-old Julia Sellman. When he returned to active duty

Captain Thomas A. Watkins: Watkins served as a civilian recruiter for Governor Hicks in 1861. At the end of the year he enlisted and was appointed captain of Company B, Purnell Legion Cavalry. In 1864 he served as Provost Marshal of Annapolis. When Companies B and C were sent to the Army of the Potomac as replacement for the Maryland Brigade, he rejoined his command. He was severely wounded in the August battle for the Weldon Railroad. Discharged in December of 1864, Thomas Watkins was murdered by Captain John H. Boyle CSA on March 24, 1865. (D.C.T.)

he was made inspecting officer of all troops in and around Annapolis. This was followed by his appointment to Provost Marshal of the city of Annapolis. Watkins could have easily maintained this position of comfort and political importance until the end of the war. Instead he chose service in the field.

While Captain Watkins was on special assignment in Annapolis, Company B served in different areas of Baltimore until April when it was transferred to General Tyler's First Separate Brigade with headquarters at Relay. Tyler's area of operation was Fort Dix at Relay, Monrovia, Chapel Point and the Baltimore and Ohio Railroad as far west as Monocacy Junction. Second Lieutenant Joseph S. Whittington commanded the company at this time. First Lieutenant Henry L. Clayton was serving as an Aide de Camp to General Lockwood. When the company moved to Relay, Captain Watkins requested a transfer back to his old outfit.[6]

During the summer of 1864 Grant's relentless attacks on Lee's army cost the North thousands of casualties. To replace these losses many units found themselves moving from the home front to the real front. On June 7, 1864, Special Order #155 was issued from the Army of the Potomac's headquarters.

"Captains Clayton's and Watkins' cavalry companies, of the Purnell Legion, dismounted and equipped as infantry, and now serving with the provost-marshal-general, are assigned to duty with the portion of the Purnell legion, Maryland Volunteers, attached to the Third Brigade, Second Division, Fifth Corps…"

Combined, the two companies totaled 144 men. These would be welcome replacements for the now battle hardened Maryland Brigade.[7]

Shortly after their arrival Captain Watkins and his men received their baptism of fire in an assault on the Weldon Railroad. The fighting lasted for three hours and the Maryland Brigade lost 135 men killed or wounded. One of these casualties was Captain Watkins who received a severe head wound. He was given a 20 day furlough on August 31, and returned to his home where he could be cared for by his physician father. During his recovery period at "The Locust," a Confederate guerrilla by the name of Captain John H. Boyle stole one of his horses. Captain Watkins and his brother Ben tracked the horse thief into Prince George's County where they caught him at Hardesty's store. Boyle managed to get off a shot at Ben Watkins but missed and hit his horse. The Watkins brothers then overpowered the Rebel and made him their prisoner. En route back to the Provost Marshal's office in Annapolis, Boyle slipped the ropes that bound his hands and seizing a scale weight, struck Captain Watkins in the head before making good his escape. Now suffering from multiple head wounds, the stricken officer was taken to his father's home where he convalesced until the end of October.[8]

On October 24, 1864, the term of enlistment for the Purnell Legion Infantry expired and the regiment ceased to exist. The surviving members of company B who had not completed their three-year enlistment were transferred to Company H of the Eighth Maryland Infantry Regiment. [9]

Captain Watkins did not return to the Army of the Potomac. He was posted in Annapolis until his discharge in mid-December. During this time his wife gave birth to a daughter, a joy that was tempered with numerous reports that John Boyle was planning to kill Watkins.

After his discharge, Watkins moved his family to a farm on the Patuxent River named "Val Meade." On the night of March 24, 1865, Captain Boyle entered the house through a side door and shot Captain Watkins in the chest at close range. He then stole a horse from the barn and rode off. Watkins died before receiving any medical attention. Governor Bradford personally ordered cavalry details out to hunt down the murderer. The Provost Marshal in Annapolis offered a $500 reward and requested assistance from his counterpart in Washington, D.C.[10]

Captain Thomas H. Watkins was buried with full military honors at All Hollows Church where he had married Julia fourteen months earlier. John H. Boyle was captured at Frederick, Maryland on April 15, 1865. He served time for horse stealing, but was never brought to trial for killing Watkins.[11]

COMPANY C
PURNELL LEGION
CAVALRY

When the Purnell Legion was first organized in 1861, only two companies of cavalry were authorized, namely A and B. On October 17, 1861, Colonel William H. Purnell's offer to recruit two additional companies was accepted by the Acting Secretary of War, Thomas A. Scott. Of these only Company C was actually formed.[1]

Company C was recruited in Baltimore City in September of 1862. Its line officers were Captain Theodore Clayton, First Lieutenant Charles W. Palmer, and Second Lieutenant Washington I. Purnell. Captain Clayton resigned his position as First Lieutenant and Quartermaster of the First Maryland Light Artillery on July 18 to take command of the company. Lieutenant Palmer moved up a grade when he transferred from Company B.[2]

Clayton's company served in the Defenses of Baltimore at Camp Bradford for the remainder of 1862 and early part of 1863. It then spent time at Harper's Ferry before moving to Drummondtown, Virginia, in March. On May 3 General Lockwood ordered Captain Clayton and his company of 42 men to report to Major Henry B. Judd, the post commander at Wilmington, in the District of Delaware. Company C remained there for the balance of 1863. Captain Clayton was detailed to Baltimore City by General Schenck on June

2, and did not return to his company until July 28.[3]

On April 6, 1864, a state election was held in Maryland. To prevent any disorderly conduct at the polling places in Somerset and Worcester counties, Brigadier General John R. Kenly took Company D of the First Delaware Cavalry and 20 men from Company C under Orderly Sergeant Joseph L. Janney to Salisbury. They arrived by special train from Wilmington on the evening on the fifth. The next day General Kenly dispersed the Delaware cavalry and men from the First Eastern Shore Infantry Regiment throughout the counties with orders to remain one mile outside the election precincts and notify the judges of their presence, but not to enter the polling places unless summoned by them. The men of the Purnell Legion detail were utilized as couriers. Only in Nutter's and Colbourne's districts of Worcester County were the soldiers called in to the polling places. By midnight all the detachments had returned to Salisbury and Kenly returned to Wilmington with his men the next day.[4]

In January Captain Clayton was again detached from his company and ordered to Baltimore City, this time to serve as an Assistant Inspector in the Eighth Army Corps. On June 2, he was made Commissary of Substance at the Second Division Hospital of the Fifth Army Corps.[5]

On May 16, General Kenly was ordered to send Company C of the Purnell Legion and a company of infantry from the First Eastern Shore Regiment by train to Baltimore. "Issue 150 rounds of ammunition and five days rations. A company of militia will be sent to you to-morrow." This move was preparatory to Company C's joining the Army of the Potomac. As with Company B, Company C joined the Purnell Legion Infantry Regiment serving in the Maryland Brigade and fought through the Siege of Petersburg and the attacks on the Weldon Railroad. [6]

In late October of 1864 the three-year term of enlistment came to an end for the Purnell Infantry Regiment. Because the men of Company C had enlisted a year later than those of companies A and B, they were transferred to Company I of the Eighth Maryland Infantry Regiment to serve out their term of service. Captain Clayton did not wish to see his men officially termed infantry and "Resigned on account of the transfer of the enlisted men of his command from cavalry to the infantry arm of the service…" He was granted a discharge on December 10, 1864, and left the service on December 17.[7]

FIRST POTOMAC HOME BRIGADE CAVALRY (COLE'S)

I n 1861 a special force was authorized to protect the border between Maryland and Virginia, and the Baltimore and Ohio Railroad which connected the Nation's Capital with the West. The original plan called for one infantry brigade of four regiments with one company of cavalry assigned to each regiment. Only three regiments of infantry were recruited and the brigade formation abandoned. The four companies of orphaned cavalry were eventually formed into a battalion under the command of senior captain Henry A. Cole. Cole was promoted to major and the unit designated First Potomac Home Brigade Cavalry. In 1864 the battalion was expanded to a full regiment. Regardless of its size, it was most often referred to simply as Cole's Cavalry.[1]

During most of its active service the First Potomac Home Brigade Cavalry was assigned to the Department of West Virginia. Its nominal base of operations was Harper's Ferry and much of its combat experience took place in that vicinity on both sides of the Potomac River. It also served stints in the Army of the Potomac, General John Pope's short lived Army of Virginia, Sheridan's Army of the Shenandoah, and the Middle Department. By the end of the war these blue horsemen had covered 7,000 miles from Gettysburg to the James River, up and down the Shenandoah Valley and deep into West Virginia as far as the Kentucky border.[2]

At the beginning of the war former Maryland Governor and Congressman Francis Thomas was instrumental in securing the authorization for the creation of the Potomac Home Brigade. His efforts at recruiting led to the formation of three infantry regiments and four companies of cavalry during the summer and fall of 1861. The first company of cavalry, Company A, was from Frederick. It was commanded by Captain Henry A. Cole. Company B was raised in Cumberland and commanded by Captain William Firey. Company C under Captain John Horner came from Emmitsburg and Gettysburg. Captain Pierce K. Keirl recruited Company D in Howard County and Baltimore City.[3]

At the beginning of the war many of the Union cavalrymen were city boys who had to learn how to ride and shoot. They were inferior to their Confederate counterparts. This was not the case with Cole's men. Recruited mostly from the farms of the Western Maryland region, they knew how to ride and were skilled in the use of weapons. Young single men for the most part, they made excellent troopers from the beginning and proved to be a match for their Southern foes.[4]

When fully recruited, equipped and trained, Company B was assigned to duty in West Virginia while the other three companies patrolled the Potomac River from Frederick to Cumberland, Maryland. Duty during the winter of 1862 proved to be largely routine. In early January Cole's Cavalry participated in the repulse of a Confederate crossing of the Potomac River and a skirmish at Hancock on the first and second of January. When the Confederates retired to Winchester to take up winter quarters, a detachment followed to learn their strength and location.[5]

The spring of 1862 witnessed the stolen whiskey incident. A barrel of whiskey was safely locked up in the provost marshal's office with a guard posted at the door. Some of Cole's ingenious troopers sneaked into the basement through a rear window and, with a long auger, bored a hole through the floor and the bottom of the barrel. The whiskey was caught in camp kettles, which were then passed out the basement window and quickly disappeared. The provost marshal was not amused.[6]

In March Cole's Cavalry led the advance of General Nathaniel P. Banks' Division across the Potomac River and into the Shenandoah Valley. Skirmishes were fought at Martinsburg, Bloomer's Gap, Bunker Hill, Stevenson's Depot, and Winchester. The battalion suffered its first casualties in an engagement between Bunker Hill and Winchester for which it received a written commendation from its brigade commander, General A. S. Williams.

In the latter part of March Companies A and C went with Williams' Brigade to join General Irving McDowell's Corps in Eastern Virginia. Companies B and D remained at Winchester with the division commanded by General James Shields. They took part in the Battle of Kernstown on March 22, 1862. The other two companies returned in time to join in the pursuit of the retreating Confederates. Elements of the battalion saw action during April and May at Edinburg, Grass Lick, Wardensburg, and Charlestown.[7]

After the defeat of General John Pope's Army of Virginia at the Second Battle of Bull Run in August, Robert E. Lee launched the first Confederate invasion of the North, which culminated in the Battle of Antietam on September 17. Still in the Shenandoah Valley, Cole's Cavalry scouted the Confederate advance. Skirmishes were fought at Leesburg, Virginia; at Edwards Ferry on the Potomac River; and in Maryland at Monocacy Creek and Lovettsville. Their casualties were 3 killed and 9 wounded. Cole's men took 35 prisoners.[8]

The Confederate army crossed into Maryland above and below Harper's Ferry and concentrated at Frederick City. Harper's Ferry remained in Federal hands with a garrison of 12,000 men under the command of Colonel Dixon S. Miles. Realizing the threat this posed to his supply lines, Lee sent two thirds of his army under Stonewall Jackson to capture the post. Lee went to Hagerstown with General Longstreet and left a thin screen of troops to cover the passes in South Mountain until the army could be reunited.[9]

Cole's Cavalry had returned to Harper's Ferry and were now part of the doomed garrison. Major Cole and Captain Charles Russell of the First Maryland Cavalry Regiment volunteered to go through the Confederate lines and report the condition of things to General McCellan who had reached Frederick with the Army of the Potomac. Taking separate routes, both men were successful, but Colonel Miles decided to surrender the town before either man could return with a reply.[10]

With surrender near at hand, the commanders of the various cavalry units at Harper's Ferry requested permission to fight their way out through the enemy lines. Miles reluctantly agreed and orders were issued to leave on the night of September 14. Due to their thorough knowledge of the area, Cole's Cavalry was chosen to lead the approximately 1,500 cavalrymen through the dark to safety. Lieutenant Hanson Green, with three men from Company A, formed the advanced guard for the column.

Riding through the night with scabbards tied to their saddles to muffle the noise, the troopers proceeded along the riverbank, crossed the Chesapeake and Ohio Canal, and made their way across country. Just before dawn they captured an ammunition train belonging to Longstreet's Corps. En route to Pennsylvania one of the wagons broke an axle. The Marylanders covered the ammunition with hay and set it on fire causing a terrific explosion. [11]

During the month of October General J.E.B. Stuart led his cavalry on a raid completely around the Army of the Potomac. Cole's battalion followed their trail giving progress reports to the Federal cavalry commander and capturing seven Confederate troopers in a skirmish at Hyattstown.[12]

In November the First Maryland Battalion was assigned to the Twelfth Corps. The only cavalry unit with the corps, it was heavily engaged in scouting, screening, and skirmishing. When one of the divisions made a reconnaissance up the Shenandoah Valley, Cole's men accompanied it and fought skirmishes at Charlestown, Berryville, and Winchester. When the Twelfth Corps was transferred east at the end of December, Cole's Cavalry remained in the valley.[13]

In June of 1863 the battalion was involved in the early movements of the second Confederate invasion of the North which crested at the battle of Gettysburg. General Robert H. Milroy's division had been sent up the Shenandoah Valley to establish a base of operations at Winchester. On June 13 Cole's Cavalry encountered the advance of a full division of Confederate cavalry in Milroy's rear near Berryville. Couriers were sent through the enemy lines to warn him of the threatened encirclement. Nonetheless, Milroy was defeated at the Second Battle of Winchester, June 14–15. The battalion served as a rear guard during the Federal retreat. Fighting at Williamsport, Catoctin Creek and Frederick, they were the last Union troops to cross the Potomac River.[14]

Two officers and three ladies: (L) Captain Albert Hunter, Company C, and (R) Captain Daniel Link, Company A, Cole's Cavalry, had their photograph taken at Marken's Gallery in Frederick. Note the way the two men have crossed their legs at the ankle. The identities of the ladies are unknown, but appear in other views from the same photograph album.

Daniel Link enlisted as a private on August 10, 1861. He was promoted to sergeant, lieutenant, and, finally, captain on March 11, 1864. Link was mustered out on January 23, 1865.

Albert Hunter entered the service as a bugler on September 1, 1861. He was promoted to Second Lieutenant on November 20, 1861 and captain on June 10, 1862. Captured once during the war, he was discharged on September 9, 1864. (D.C.T.)

As the Army of Northern Virginia advanced once more through Maryland on its way to Pennsylvania, Cole's Cavalry reversed roles and practiced partisan warfare against the invading Confederate army. The battalion was constantly engaged during the latter half of June and suffered numerous casualties in actions at Martinsburg, Williamsport, Catoctin Creek and Frederick City, where it drove the First Maryland Cavalry CSA out of town to the cheers of the loyal citizens there.[15]

The battalion did not serve as a unit during the battle of Gettysburg. Due to their knowledge of the area, its men were distributed through the Union army as guides, scouts, and couriers. At Fountain Head, Pennsylvania, a detachment under Lieutenant Horner captured a courier with orders from General Lee to General Ewell. This information was delivered to General Reynolds, the first Union corps commander on the field at Gettysburg. After the battle Cole's men followed and harassed the Confederate army as it retreated back into Virginia. When the Gettysburg Campaign was concluded, intensive recruiting took place to refill the ranks depleted by such strenuous service.[16]

In the latter half of 1863 the battalion was headquartered at Harper's Ferry and spent most of its time scouting the Shenandoah Valley. During a typical reconnaissance mission each of the four companies would leave camp by a different route and rendezvous several days later as far as 100 miles from their starting point. They frequently clashed with Mosby's command. On one such occasion Mosby was forced to abandon his horse and escape capture by climbing up the side of a mountain. He wrote in his memoirs that forty years after the war his hat was returned to him by a niece of "Lieutenant Colonel Cole of the regiment that captured it." Mosby's biographer described Cole as an "ambitious" officer and *The Baltimore Sun* wrote of him,"…he is the same value to us that White and Mosby are to the rebels." [17]

In October a detail under the command of Captain Frank Gallagher went to Berryville to ascertain the strength of the Confederate force there. The captain, wrapped in a great coat to conceal his uniform, met with the loyal owner of a local hotel. In a dining room filled with Confederate soldiers, he was briefed on troop dispositions in the area. Although subsequently hampered by a broken leg from the kick of a horse, Captain Gallagher and his men made it safely back to their lines with the information.[18]

The Ninth Maryland Infantry Regiment was stationed at Charlestown at this time. On October 19, Imboden's cavalry brigade attacked the regiment. A relief force led by Cole's Cavalry arrived too late to save the Ninth Maryland. The battalion repeatedly attacked the Confederates as they withdrew with their prisoners and suffered heavy casualties in the process. Private Newcomer, the regimental historian, was knocked from his horse by a bullet, which grazed his head and shot off the front of his hat. He remounted and joined the charge.[19]

In December Cole's Cavalry participated in a 15 day raid up the Shenandoah Valley. Fighting took place at Upperville, Edinburg, New Market, Harrisonburg, and Staunton. This was a demonstration in support of another cavalry force cutting the railroad from Lynchburg to Bristol, Tennessee, in an attempt to delay Confederate reinforcements from being sent to the Western theatre.[20]

January 10, 1864, was a bitter cold night and the ground was snow covered. The battalion was in winter quarters on Loudon Heights opposite Harper's Ferry. The troopers normally slept fully dressed with their weapons near at hand, but on this night had relaxed somewhat in view of the extreme weather and partially disrobed when they retired to the warmth of their tents. About 3 o'clock in the morning they were awakened by a gunshot—the camp was under attack by Mosby's Rangers!

One of Mosby's scouts, a man named Stringfellow, was a resident of the area who had infiltrated the camp and presented a plan of attack to Mosby. The objective was to capture Major Cole who was disliked as much by the Confederates as Mosby was by the Federals. Part of Mosby's command entered the camp on foot in what proved to be an unsuccessful attempt to seize Cole's men as they emerged from their tents. Alerted by gunfire, the blue troopers snatched up their weapons and rushed out into the snowy night, some clad only in their underclothes, as Stringfellow and a group of mounted men charged into the camp.

In spite of the darkness and surprise, Cole's men more than held their own. Federal fire erupted from the headquarters building and the adjacent barn. Captain Vernon rallied his company in the rear of the camp and fought furiously. Seasoned veterans that they were, the Yankees did not attempt to mount their horses so that they could fire at any mounted man in the darkness without fear of hitting one of their comrades. A Confederate officer called out to his men to set fire to the tents and shoot by the light of the flames. These were his last words as he fell dead seconds later. Trooper Newcomer wrote that after the fight he searched the body of a lieutenant lying in front of his tent and found he was also a Baltimorean. After the war he was able to return to the family a photograph of the officer's sister that he carried at the time of his death.

The attempt to capture Major Cole failed. He was quartered in a house on the edge of the camp. As the Confederates entered the front door, the major went out the back and within seconds was in the midst of the melee rallying his men. After a spirited battle Mosby gave up the fight and retreated, pursued by Cole's men until they lost the trail at the river's edge.[21]

Cole's commanding officer praised the battalion's stout defense and his commendation went up the chain of command to the General in Chief who sent the following telegram—a most unusual recognition for a mere cavalry battalion.

Washington, D.C., January 20, 1864
Brig. Gen. B.F. Kelly
Cumberland, Md.

GENERAL. I have just received from your headquarters Maj. Henry A. Cole's report of the repulse
of Mosby's attack upon his camp at Loudoun Heights
on the 10th instant. Major Cole and his command,
the battalion of Potomac Home Brigade Cavalry,
Maryland Volunteers, deserve high praise for their
gallantry in repelling this rebel assault.
Very respectfully, your obedient servant
H.W. Halleck
General-in-Chief"[22]

Casualties were severe on both sides, Mosby lost 4 killed, including 2 offi-cers, 7 wounded, and 1 captured. The losses among Cole's men were 4 killed and 17 wounded. Captain George W. F. Vernon of Company A suffered a serious head wound which resulted in the loss of an eye. He eventually returned to duty and served until the end of the rebellion. After the war the veterans of Cole's Cavalry held their annual reunion on the same date as the attack on the camp, January 10. On one occasion they even invited John S. Mosby to be their guest.[23]

Mosby's biographer wrote that "...no setback in Mosby's career had been or would be as costly as that at Loudon Heights," and noted that this was the opinion of General Stuart and other officers. A member of Stuart's staff states that the abortive attack was Mosby's "...only serious failure."[24]

Cole's Cavalry clashed again with Mosby on January 16 at Leesburg and February 20 at Upperville. After this most of the men re-enlisted and were granted 30-day furloughs. The battalion returned to Frederick and was given an enthusiastic welcome by the predominantly loyal population of that city. The troopers were officially greeted by the city fathers amid cheering and flag waving by the citizens and the ringing of church and fire bells. After a formal ceremony and banquet at the city hall, the troopers disbursed to their homes to enjoy their furlough.[25]

At this time the battalion was recruited to full regimental strength with the addition of companies E through M constituting two additional battalions. Major Cole was advanced to the rank of colonel on April 20, 1864. George W. F. Vernon became his second in command with the rank of lieutenant colonel. The battalion commanders were majors Flory, Mooney, and Horner.[26]

During the remainder of 1864 the First Regiment Potomac Home Brigade Cavalry saw almost continuous service in the field. In addition to numerous scouting expeditions and skirmishes with Mosby and other Confederate cavalry units, Cole's Cavalry participated in all three of the campaigns in the Shenandoah Valley. The first of these was the advance up the valley by a small army under the command of General Franz Segal, which culminated in the battle of New Market on May 15. The battle was a Union defeat, and is remembered for the participation of the cadets from the Virginia Military Institute. The new recruits did not take part in this battle, only the original battalion which covered Segal's retreat.[27]

General Segal was replaced by General David Hunter who carried out the Lynchburg Campaign. The veterans of the original battalion led Hunter's

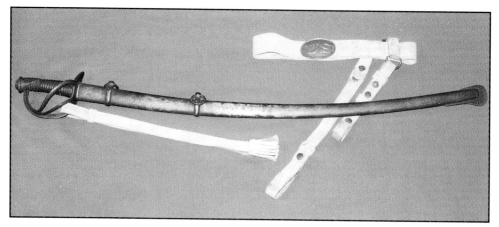

Corporal William N. Currens:
A carpenter from Taneytown, Currens enlisted as a private in Company C of Cole's Cavalry on August 27, 1861. He was promoted to regimental commissary sergeant on September 1, 1864. Records show that Currens received an additional 40 cents a day for the use of his own horse and equipment. After the war Currens moved to Indiana where he joined Encampment #80 of the Union Veteran Legion.

With this photograph are shown Currens' saber, belt, and oval U.S. belt plate. The Dragoon model 1839 enlisted man's saber belt is made of white buff leather. It is a rare example of Mexican War "war surplus." It was probably taken from the Maryland Militia and issued to the volunteers of 1861. The saber is a model 1840 Heavy Cavalry Saber made by Ames, dated 1851, with a white buff sword knot. (D.C.T.)

advance up the valley. The new recruits were assigned as infantry to Colonel Mulligan's brigade, which supplied logistical support to the army. The mounted men participated in all the battles of the campaign between June 3 and June 14 including Harrisonburg, Piedmont, Staunton, Tye River, Lexington, Buckhannon, and Lynchburg. [28]

Hunter's advance stalled at Lynchburg. Low on ammunition and believing he faced superior numbers, he retreated westward through the rugged West

Virginia mountains. Cole's troopers accompanied Hunter's army and were engaged at Catawba Mountain and Salem.[29]

With the Valley unobstructed, the Second Corps of the Northern Virginia now commanded by Major General Jubal A. Early advanced toward the Potomac River and launched the third invasion of the North which resulted in the battle of Monocacy and a brief siege of the Federal capital. A portion of Cole's men returned from West Virginia and skirmished with Early's advanced elements. General William W. Averill, the Union cavalry commander in the area, suggested that Cole's men "…might be of service at departmental headquarters…they will make excellent couriers and guides." As the Confederates advanced toward Harper's Ferry they engaged Mulligan's Brigade at Leestown where the new battalions, still serving as infantry, were under fire for the first time.[30]

During the battle of Monocacy, fought on July 9, most of the regiment was stationed at Maryland Heights and in nearby Pleasant Valley. Lieutenant Colonel Vernon commanded a detachment with General Lew Wallace's force holding the line along the Monocacy River. Ordered to harass the enemy, he roved behind the Confederate lines and captured many prisoners.[31]

After the Monocacy Campaign, the regiment was attached to General George Crook's cavalry brigade in the Army of West Virginia. They were stationed principally at Hagerstown and picketed the fords along the Potomac River. Crook pursued the Confederates as they withdrew up the Shenandoah Valley until he was attacked at Kernstown and forced to retreat to Harper's Ferry. The regiment suffered heavy casualties in this engagement.[32]

The Confederates then made a number of sorties into Maryland and Pennsylvania in which the regiment was involved, including the pursuit of General John McCausland's cavalry after the burning of Chambersburg. Private Newcomer described riding through the burning city in pursuit of the raiders. Some of the recruits, who had recently joined the regiment, were not yet equipped with saddles or bridles and rode bareback with only a halter on their horses.[33]

Another Confederate sortie into Maryland in early August resulted in a fierce firefight at Keedysville, near the Antietam battlefield. The lead unit of the regiment suffered 18 casualties out of 35 men.[34]

Also in August General Philip H. Sheridan was assigned to a consolidated command in the Valley, which was named the Army of the Shenandoah. It was composed of elements from the Army of the Potomac, the Eighteenth Army Corps from Louisiana, and Crook's Department of West Virginia troops. During the ensuing weeks he conducted a successful campaign which culminated in a Federal victory at the battle of Cedar Creek on October 19 that virtually destroyed Early's army and ended major Confederate operations in the Shenandoah Valley.[35]

One of Sheridan's first acts was to reorganize his cavalry. On August 9, a new brigade was formed under the command of Colonel Charles R. Lowell, Jr., to which Cole's Cavalry was assigned. During the month of August the brigade was in almost continuous action picketing, skirmishing and conducting reconnaissance. As the two armies maneuvered for position it ranged from the Potomac River as far south as Cedar Creek. On August 26 it captured 26 prisoners at Charlestown.[36]

During this period of time Colonel Cole was on sick leave in Frederick and Major Alexander M. Florey temporarily commanded the regiment. Company I was assigned to Sheridan's headquarters on the recommendation of General John D. Stevenson, the post commander at Harper's Ferry. After the death of Colonel Lowell at the battle of Cedar Creek, his brigade was disbanded. On September 8, the regiment was directed to report to Harper's Ferry to be dismounted. The most efficient counter-Mosby force in the Union Army was being converted to infantry. Twice during the month of October General Stevenson requested that Cole's men be remounted and armed with Spencer repeating rifles for action against Mosby's Rangers. On October 30, the regiment was relieved from picket duty at Harper's Ferry and transferred to Martinsburg. Finally, in December, the regiment was given back its horses. Remounted, Cole's Cavalry spent the final months of the war in West Virginia, protecting the Baltimore and Ohio Railroad.[37]

When the First Regiment Potomac Home Brigade Cavalry was mustered out of Federal service at Harper's Ferry on June 28, 1865, it had a combat record second to none in the state of Maryland. Cole's Cavalry captured over 1,000 Confederate prisoners and inflicted and untold number of casualties on its enemy. Their success did not come without a price. Forty-seven officers and enlisted men were killed and 122 died of wounds, disease, or in Confederate prison camps. These figures are even more impressive in view of the fact that the unit consisted of only four companies until the spring of 1864 when it was enlarged to a full regiment.[38]

Henry A. Cole was a 26-year-old carpenter when he recruited Company A in his native city of Frederick. He rose from the rank of Captain to Colonel of the regiment that is synonymous with his name. Several times in 1865 he commanded a brigade in the Department of West Virginia. After the war he was employed at the United States Custom House in Baltimore. He died in 1909 at the age of 71. His body was brought to Frederick for burial in Mount Olivet Cemetery. The funeral was conducted by the Reynolds Camp Number 2 of the Grand Army of the Republic. Among the pallbearers was his second in command, George W. F. Vernon. Permanently blinded in the right eye during the fight with Mosby's Rangers on Loudon Heights in 1864, Vernon became a successful patent attorney and co-editor of the *History and Roster of Maryland Volunteers War of 1861-65* published by the State of Maryland in 1898.[39]

Death of Summers: James E. Taylor's sketch of the encounter between Captain George D. Summers of Company F, Second Potomac Home Brigade and Major Harry Gilmor of the Second Maryland Cavalry C.S.A. The action took place at Summit Point in October of 1863. (Western Reserve Historical Society, Cleveland, Ohio)

SECOND POTOMAC HOME BRIGADE COMPANY F (MOUNTED)

During the first year of the war three regiments of infantry were raised in the western counties of the state with the special designation Potomac Home Brigade. Company F of the Second Regiment was recruited at Hancock in Washington County in August and September of 1861. Its first officers were Captain Lewis Dysche, First Lieutenant George P. Summers, and Second Lieutenant Norval McKinley.[1]

On September 7, 1862 Lieutenant Summers tended his resignation stating, "Some of the men and Second Lt. in two instances has got drunk and acted disgracefully and were not punished by our Captain." When Summers did not receive a response he wrote directly to his regimental commander, Colonel Robert Bruce, requesting assistance in obtaining his discharge. Colonel Bruce replied the next day and informed Summers that Captain Dysche was also seeking his discharge and he, Bruce, "...knows of no better person to take command of the company than yourself." Dysche did resign on October 25, 1862, and Summers was appointed captain of Company F on December 8, 1862.[2]

Returns for the Middle Department, Eighth Army Corps dated January 31, 1863, show Company F as part of the Garrison at Martinsburg. On May 16 of the same year Summers' Cavalry was captured at Charlestown, WV. The next day General Milroy sent Captain James R. Utt with companies D and E of the Third West Virginia Cavalry and a detachment of the Thirteenth Pennsylvania towards Front Royal in an attempt rescue them. Utt's force intercepted the Rebels at Piedmont Station. In a short, but bloody, battle about 50 men and horses were recaptured and 40 of the enemy made prisoners. Two of the enemy were killed as were Captain Utt and Sergeant Graham of the Thirteenth Pennsylvania.[3]

In June of 1863 the Army of Northern Virginia moved through the lower end of the Shenandoah Valley pushing the remnants of Milroy's command north after capturing Winchester on June 15. Company F skirmished with the advancing Confederates at Berryville on the 14th. One man was wounded and 2 captured before they fell back through Charlestown and then Halltown. On the June 16, Captain Summers lead his company across the river to Maryland Heights "...being the last soldier in this command to leave Dixie."

On June 17, General E. B. Tyler ordered Company F and Captain Vernon's Company A of Cole's Cavalry to Point of Rocks to hold that position against the advancing enemy. Simultaneously, Colonel E. B. White's Forty Third Battalion of Virginia Cavalry crossed the Potomac River below Berlin (now Brunswick) with the intention of attacking the camp of Mean's Loundon County Rangers at that same location. They struck the Union cavalry en route to the Point. Summers reported after the battle, "Before we got there we were attacked by White's battalion and were over powered and whipped." [4]

The next day Major Harry Gilmor and the First Maryland Cavalry CSA were ordered by General Richard Ewell to move from Boonsboro to Frederick and, if possible, destroy the railroad bridge at Monocacy Junction. A detachment from Vernon's and Summers' companies skirmished with Gilmor's advanced troopers and pushed them back on the main body. Gilmor then dismounted 20 men with rifles and skirmished with the Union cavalry at long range. He followed this up with a charge that drove the Yankees through the streets of Frederick City and out along the road to Harper's Ferry. Three men of Company F were captured and one Confederate soldier wounded.[5]

For the balance of the month of June Company F operated between Berlin, Maryland Heights and Frederick City. On July 12, the company was temporarily attached to Cole's Battalion of Maryland Cavalry.[6]

By the end of August, Company F had regained its independent status and was part of the First Brigade of the Maryland Heights Division commanded by General Henry H. Lockwood. Returning from a scout late on the night of September 28, Summers reported to his brigade commander, Colonel George D. Weels, that a force of 500 men from the Twelfth Virginia Cavalry and Gilmor's Battalion were near Winchester. He added "...that with a force of 250 men he could find and whip them." For Summers his clash with Gilmor would come soon enough.[7]

In early October Company F was ordered to accompany the Ninth Maryland Infantry Regiment to Charlestown to act as an early warning station for the garrison at Harper's Ferry. At this same time Harry Gilmor, now a lieutenant colonel commanding the Second Maryland Battalion, was operating in the area with about 50 men. Learning that a Union cavalry force half his size was on the road to Smithfield, Gilmor pursued Company F through Smithfield and beyond Summit Point. After a futile cross country chase, Gilmor returned to Summit Point to water his horses at the "White House" owned by a man named Morrow. While his men were dismounted Summers' detachment happened upon the grounded Rebels and opened fire. One of Gilmor's men, a man named Ford from Baltimore, was shot through the head. As soon as the firing broke out Gilmor ordered ten of his men with carbines to take shelter in a stone stable and hold the Yankees off until he could get some of his men mounted. Taking aim at the officer leading the Union charge, Gilmor fired and Summers fell to the ground. The bullet had struck the side of his nose and passed out the back of his head.

Gilmor then joined his mounted men and counter charged Company F. The Union cavalry were stuck between two post and rail fences that lined the road and unable to deploy in strength. Leaderless and taking more fire than it could give; it soon gave way and was pursued along the road to Charlestown losing 23 men and 29 horses in their flight. Gilmor's losses were 1 killed, 3 wounded, and 1 captured. Captain George D. Summers was the only commissioned officer in the entire Second Regiment Potomac Home Brigade to be killed in action during the war.[8]

The survivors of Company F were with the Ninth Maryland Infantry Regiment at Charlestown when Colonel Simpson sent a force of about 50 men to Berryville, Smithfield and Summit Point under the command of Lieutenant Aquilla S. Gallion. Gallion had enlisted in Company F as a private in 1861 and, at the age of 44, was promoted to Second Lieutenant on December 9, 1862. The Union reconnaissance force encountered White's Battalion of Virginia Cavalry at Berryville consisting of 330 men both mounted and fighting as infantry. The Union cavalry charged and drove a small number of the enemy out of town on the Millwood Road until they came upon White's main force. The Confederates then returned the compliment and pursued Gallion's command for a distance of 4 or 5 miles. Four of the Marylanders horses gave out and they were forced to attempt their escape on foot. One was wounded and taken prisoner. Another reached Charlestown on the morning of the October 18 and was in the act of warning Lieutenant Gallion of the enemy's approach when firing broke out and the pickets were driven in.[9]

Lieutenant Norval McKinley assumed command of Company F after the death of Summers. By the end of 1863 Company F was assigned to the cavalry brigade of Colonel William H. Boyd in the Department of West Virginia. On January 31,1864, Company F moved to Winchester with a mixed force of cavalry and artillery under the command of Lt. Colonel Charles Fitz Simmon, Third New York Cavalry. Company F was again assigned to Cole's Cavalry along with detachments from the Sixth Michigan and First Connecticut cavalry regiments, numbering in all about 225 men. At Blue's Gap this force skirmished with Rosser's command on February 1. The Seventh Virginia Regiment lost 7 men killed, wounded, or captured. The only Union loss was one man wounded in Company F.[10]

In September of 1864 the original members of the company were discharged having completed their three years of service. The remaining veterans and new recruits under Captain McKinley continued to serve in the Cavalry Division of the Department of West Virginia. In 1865 the surviving members of Company F were transferred to infantry companies in the Second Potomac Home Brigade Regiment before being mustered out on May 29, 1864.[11]

SMITH'S INDEPENDENT COMPANY OF MARYLAND CAVALRY

Only two companies of Maryland soldiers were enlisted to serve as independent companies and remained so until the end of the war. The first was the Patapsco Guard from Howard County. The second was Smith's Cavalry Company. Ironically the Patapsco Guard spent most of its time in Pennsylvania. Smith's Company went in the opposite direction, pulling duty stations in the Eastern Shore counties of Maryland and Virginia, with only a few excursions west of the Chesapeake Bay.

On September 1, 1862, Captain George W. P. Smith was authorized to raise an independent company of cavalry. The company was mustered into Federal service on October 15 with the caveat that, "…when accepted, will be assigned to special duty in Worcester County unless the exigency of the service should require it to be consolidated or attached to some regiment for general service."[1]

Captain Smith was a 39-year-old lawyer when he enlisted at Snow Hill. First Lieutenant Authur J. Wallis entered the service on the same day. They joined Second Lieutenant Charles F. Fosler who had enlisted on September 1. The company was stationed at Snow Hill and New Town during the final months of 1862.[2]

Throughout 1863 the company was brigaded with the First and Second Eastern Shore Infantry regiments and the three companies of Purnell Legion Cavalry under the command of Brigadier General Henry H. Lockwood of Delaware. Their mission was to disrupt recruiting activities by Southern sympathizers in the state and pursue blockade-runners on the lower Potomac River.[3]

In the spring of 1863 the company began to move about the Eastern Shore counties of Maryland and Virginia. On April 8 it went to Drummondtown, Virginia, and the next day to Pungoteague. On April 11 it began a 180 mile march to Point Lookout, Maryland, where it remained throughout the months of May and June. It then moved to Eastville. While there a squad of 12 men commanded by a noncommissioned officer was detailed to Hog Island.[4]

On September 26, Captain Smith wrote a letter to Major General R. E. Schenck requesting a leave of absents to finalize several matters in relation to his law practice. Having been in the service for thirteen months he informed the general, "I gave up a large practice in the Circuit Court of the 8th Judicial Circuit of Maryland when I organized my command and the young man I left in my office is not equal to the task…" His request was initially denied because it would have left only one officer with the company. The problem was soon rectified with the promotion of First Sergeant Joseph T. Fearing to Second Lieutenant to fill the vacancy caused by the resignation of Lieutenant Wallis.

The first day of November Captain Smith wrote a letter to Lieutenant Colonel William H. Cheseborough, A.A.G. of the Eighth Army Corps, explaining this new development and headed off to Baltimore City. The next day General E. B. Tyler ordered his arrest and charged "…he is in this city without proper authority." As in many instances, no action was taken and Smith returned to duty.[5]

Smith's company spent the last two months of 1863 back in Drummondtown, Virginia. Lieutenant Fearing commanded the company while Captain Smith was detailed to court-martial duty in Baltimore until June of 1864.[6]

VOLUNTEER ENLISTMENT.

STATE OF *Maryland*   TOWN OF *Snow Hill*

I, *Francis A. White* born in *Worcester Co* in the State of *Maryland* aged *25* years, and by occupation a *house Carpenter* Do HEREBY ACKNOWLEDGE to have volunteered this *20th* day of *September* 1862 to serve as a **Soldier** in the Army of the United States of America, for the period of *THREE YEARS*, unless sooner discharged by proper authority: Do also agree to accept such bounty, pay, rations, and clothing, as are, or may be, established by law for volunteers. And I, *Francis A White* do solemnly swear, that I will bear true faith and allegiance to the **United States of America**, and that I will serve them honestly and faithfully against all their enemies or opposers whomsoever; and that I will observe and obey the orders of the President of the United States, and the orders of the officers appointed over me, according to the Rules and Articles of War.

Sworn and subscribed to, at *Snow Hill* this *20th* day of *Sept* 1862 *Francis X A. White* mark

I CERTIFY, ON HONOR, That I have carefully examined the above named Volunteer, agreeably to the General Regulations of the Army, and that in my opinion he is free from all bodily defects and mental infirmity, which would, in any way, disqualify him from performing the duties of a soldier.

EXAMINING SURGEON.

I CERTIFY, ON HONOR, That I have minutely inspected the Volunteer, *Francis A White* previously to his enlistment, and that he was entirely sober when enlisted; that, to the best of my judgment and belief, he is of lawful age; and that, in accepting him as duly qualified to perform the duties of an able-bodied soldier, I have strictly observed the Regulations which govern the recruiting service. This soldier has *hazel* eyes, *brown* hair, *fair* complexion, is *6* feet *1/4* inches high.

Capt. Smith 2nd Cavalry company
Regiment of *Md*, Volunteers,
RECRUITING OFFICER.

GOV. PRINT. OFF. Dec. 1861.

Enlistment Paper: Private Francis A. White was inducted into Federal service with this document. It contains his name, place of birth—Worcester County, occupation—carpenter, and place of enlistment—Snow Hill. The volunteer was examined for physical defects by either a surgeon (paragraph 2) or the Recruiting Officer (paragraph 3). The reversed side contained a signature block for "Consent in case of a minor." The document was signed twice in the appropriated places by Captain George W. P. Smith. Private White made his "X." White enlisted in Smith's Independent Company of Cavalry on September 20, 1862. He is listed in the *Roster of Maryland Volunteers* as having deserted on February 14, 1864, one of eight men in the company to do so. (D.C.T.)

The company remained on the Eastern Shore throughout the summer months of 1864, changing its headquarters to Salisbury in early July. Captain Smith did not return to his command until July 9.[7]

On August 13, Captain Smith reported to Captain George V. Massey, the Assistant Adjutant General, that Pocomoke Sound and the Annemesses were swarming with pirates and blockade-runners. The day before Corporal Paradise and three men captured four boats and took six prisoners. Among these was the noted deserter Stewart Tingle. The next day the prisoners' friends recaptured three of the boats and took two men of Smith's Company prisoners. They were privates Jerry Smith and Littleton Davis.[8]

In September the company was ordered across the Chesapeake Bay and arrived in Baltimore City on the night of the twelfth. During the first week of October Mosby was reported to be leading a large-scale raid near the Potomac River with 800 men and four pieces of artillery. General E. B. Tyler responded by sending four guns and all available cavalry to Rockville. The only enemy force to actually enter the state was a group of seven men led by Lieutenant Walter Bowie from Company F of Mosby's command. Bowie's men robbed a store at Sandy Springs and Bowie was tracked down and killed by the normally peaceful Quakers who owned the store.[9]

General Tyler ordered Lieutenant Vincent and 50 men of Smith's Cavalry to proceed through Ellicott Mills to Sandy Springs and cooperate with Lieutenant Colonel Knight of the First Delaware Cavalry in capturing the guerrillas. Returning from their first "combat mission" Smith's Company remained at Relay until the end of October when it was sent to Barnsville until the end of the year.[10]

The company returned to Salisbury in January of 1865. In February a force of 150 Confederates were reported to have crossed the Chesapeake Bay to the Eastern Shore of Virginia. General Halleck ordered General W. W. Morris, commanding the defenses of Baltimore, to counter the move with a land force while the United States Navy cut off their escape route. Morris sent Smith's Cavalry, but they did not arrive in time to engage the enemy.[11]

In January of 1865 Captain Smith suffered the same fate that befell many of the officer who commanded Maryland units. He was court martialed and dishonorably discharged from the service "…for preferring frivolous charges against Lieutenant J. T. Fearring of his command by reason of personal animosity." Fortunately, on February 13 he was restored to his command by Special Order #71.[12]

In April the company was ordered to look for the steamer *Sidney Jones* supposedly carrying the guerrilla Boyle after it left Battle Creek in Calvert County. Boyle was wanted for the murder of Captain Thomas Watkins of the Purnell Legion Cavalry.[13]

On May 11, 1865, General John R. Kenly ordered Captain Smith to report the number of men in his command eligible for discharge. Their date of separation was June 17, but the post commander at Salisbury, Major George H. Hooker, wanted their discharge postponed until replacements could arrive. The influx of returning Rebel soldiers and civilians had an unsettling effect on the Eastern Shore counties at this time. Sufficient troops must have been found, because Smith's Independent Company of Cavalry was mustered out of Federal service on June 30, 1865. They had served for three years without a single day of combat.[14]

Notes

First Cavalry Regiment

1. *History and Roster*, p. 701; Typed manuscript entitled "Civil War Record of Matthew T. McClannahan
2. Company I, First Maryland Cavalry, author's collection.
   The War of the Rebellion: A Compilation of the Official Records of the Union and Confederate Armies, (Washington, D.C.: 1880-1901), 128 Volumes. Series 3, Vol. I, p.799, Hereafter cited as *OR*. All subsequent citations are from Series I unless otherwise noted. *Supplement to the Official Records of the Union and Confederate Armies*, Janet B. Hewett, ed. (Wilmington, NC: 1996), Vol. 26, Part II, p. 129. Hereafter cited as *Supplement*. All subsequent citations are from Vol. 26, Part II.
3. *OR*, Vol. 12, Part 1, pp. 738-739; *Supplement*, p. 134.
4. *History and Roster*, p. 701; *Supplement*, p. 188.
5. McHenry Howard, *Recollections of a Maryland Confederate Soldier and Staff Officer*, (Baltimore: 1914), pp. 114-115; *OR*, Vol. 12 Part I, pp. 738-739.
6. *Supplement*, p. 130.
7. Muster Roll of Company L dated August 31, 1862; *Supplement*, pp. 130, 134, 145, 162, 189.
8. *Supplement*, pp. 140, 141, 167, 177, 189.
9. *OR*, Vol. 19, Part 1, p. 545.
10. McLannahan; *History and Roster*, pp728, 731.
11. J. Thomas Scharf, *History of Western Maryland*, 1882, Vol. I, p. 238.
12. Paul R. Teetor, *A Matter of Honor*, (East Brunswick: 1982), pp.173-175; *Supplement*, p. 178.
13. *OR*, Vol. 21, pp. 31-32.
14. *OR*, Vol. 21, pp. 724-726.
15. Col. Eugene Von Keilmansegge, Compiled Military Service Record, National Archives, Washington, D.C. Research for cavalry units was done from photocopies of original files. Hereafter cited as CMSR: *OR*, Vol. 25, Part II, p. 72.
16. *Historical Times Illustrated Encyclopedia of the Civil War*, Patricia L. Faust ed. (New York: 1986), p. 721. Hereafter cited as *HTIE*; *OR*, Vol. 25 Part I, p. 173.
17. *Fairfax Downey*, pp. 87, 165.
18. *Supplement*, Vol. 5, pp. 248-251: *OR*, Vol. 42 Part I, pp. 751-753.
19. *OR*, Vol. 27, Part I, p. 951; *Supplement*, pp. 146, 152, 163, 168, 169.
20. Harry W. Pfanz, *Gettysburg: Culps Hill and Cemetery Hill*, (Chapel Hill: 1993), p. 154; *Report of the Maryland Monument Commission* (Baltimore: 1891), pp. 103-105. Hereafter referenced as *MMC*; Daniel C. Toomey, *Marylanders at Gettysburg* (Baltimore:1994), pp. 7-8.
21. W.W. Goldsborough, *The Maryland Line in the Confederate Army*, (Baltimore, 1990), pp. 283-285; Stephen Z. Starr, *The Union Cavalry in the Civil War*, (Baton Rouge: 1979), Three Volumes. Vol. I, pp. 433-434, MMC, pp. 104-105.
22. McClannahan; *Supplement*, p. 146.

23. *OR*, Vol. 29, Part I, p. 362; *Supplement*, pp. 137-153.
24. Roger D. Hunt and Jack R. Brown, *Brevet Brigadier Generals in Blue* (Gaithersburg, MD: 1990), p. 155; *History and Roster*, p.704; *Supplement*, p. 195.
25. *Supplement*, pp. 137, 195; *OR*, Vol. 33, p. 358.
26. *History and Roster*, p. 704; *OR*, Vol. 33, p. 1051; *Supplement*, p. 132.
27. *Supplement*, p. 132; *OR*, Vol. 36, p. 634; *OR*, Vol. 40 Part II, p. 48.
28. *OR*, Vol. 40 ,Part II, pp. 399, 552.
29. *OR*, Vol. 42, Part I, p. 381; *Supplement*, p. 132.
30. McClannahan; *Supplement*, pp.138, 154.
31. *OR*, Vol. 42 Part II, pp. 908-910, 1061, 1081; Part III, pp. 67, 233, 468.
32. *Supplement*, pp. 148, 155, 161, 171, 175, 181.
33. *History and Roster*, p. 702; *OR*, Vol. 46, Part III, p.1033; *Supplement*, pp. 171, 175, 176.

Second Cavalry Regiment

1. *History and Roster*, p. 748.
2. *OR*, Vol. 27, Part II, p. 811; *OR*, Vol. 29, Part II, p. 612; *History and Roster*, pp. 748-749.
3. "The Battle of Monocacy: One Soldier's Story," Richard E. Clem, *Maryland Cracker Barrel*, June 1989 pp. 11, 12.
4. Captain William F. Bragg CMSR.
5. *Civil War Interments at the Annapolis National Cemetery*, (Annapolis: N.D.), compiled by Jack Kelbaugh and privately published, pp. 20, 70, 104, 110, 124.126.
6. Private William H. Stone CMSR.
7. *History and Roster*, p. 748.

Third Cavalry Regiment

1. *History and Roster*, p. 757;
2. Colonel Charles C. Tavis, CMSR; Joseph Balkoski, *Beyond the Beach Head*, (Harrisburg: 1989), pp. 169, 179.
3. *HTIE*, p. 296.
4. *OR*, Series III Vol. 4, p. 1203; *History and Roster*, p. 757; Tavis, CMSR.
5. *OR*, Vol. 29, Part II, pp. 399, 524, 569.
6. *Kent County 1628-1980*, (Perry Publications: 1980), p. 18.
7. Tavis, CMSR.
8. *Supplement*, pp. 233-237.
9. *Supplement, pp. 241-242, 248, 250*; The Baltimore *American March 22, 1864*.
10. Richard B. Irwin, *History of the 19th Army Corps*, (New York: 1892), pp. 280, 289; *OR*, Vol. 34, Part II, pp. 613, 727, 770.
11. *OR*, Vol. 34, Part IV, p. 29; *Supplement*, p. 242; Tavis CMSR.
12. General Order No. 81 issued July 2, 1864; Tavis CMSR.
13. Hunt, p. 607; Tavis CMSR.
14. *Supplement*, pp. 239-240, 243, 250-250, 250, 256.
15. *OR*, Vol. 34, Part IV, pp. 425, 426; *OR*, Vol. 41, Part II, pp. 66, 66-70.
16. *OR*, Vol. 41, Part IV, pp. 366, 977.
17. *History and Roster*, p.757.

18. *OR*, Vol. 49, Part I, pp. 109, 749.
19. *History and Roster*, p. 757; *OR*, Vol. 49, p. 1109.

Purnell Legion Cavalry Company A

1. *OR*, Vol. 5, p. 22; Duvall File.
2. *OR*, Vol. 51, Part 1, p. 518.
3. *Supplement*, Vol. 26, p. 258.
4. *OR*, Vol. 27, Part 3, p. 262.
5. *Report of the State of Maryland Gettysburg Monument Commission*, (Baltimore: 1891), pp. 102-103; hereafter referenced as MMC.

Purnell Legion Cavalry Company B

1. Kelbaugh, News Letter; Roster p. 785.
2. *Supplement*, Vol. 26, pp. 260-261.
3. *OR*, Vol. 19, Part 2, p.338; *Supplement*, Vol. 26 p. 261; Watkins File.
4. Original letter in the Union Room Collection of the Maryland National Guard Military Historical Society. Here after referenced as URC.
5. *OR*, Vol. 27, Part 3, pp. 638, 810; Vol. 29 part 2 p. 134, *Supplement*, Vol. 26 p.261.
6. Kelbaugh; *OR*, Vol. 33, p. 1051, Watkins File.
7. *OR*, Vol. 36, Part 3, pp. 669, 739.
8. Kelbaugh; Watkins File.
9. Roster pp. 785-790, 787, 788.
10. Kelbaugh; Watkins File.
11. Kelbaugh.

Purnell Legion Cavalry Company C

1. *OR*, Series III, Vol. 1 pp. 502, 578.
2. Captain Theodore Clayton CMSR; *History and Roster*; 1 p. 787.
3. *OR*, Vol. 19, Part II, p. 383; *OR*, Vol. 25 Part II, p.33; *OR*, Vol. 29 part II, pp.35, 611; *OR*, Vol. 33, p. 476; Captain Theodore Clayton CMSR.
4. *OR*, Vol. 33, pp. 826-827.
5. Captain Theodore Clayton CMSR.
6. *OR*, Vol. 36, Part II, pp. 802, 832.
7. *History and Roster*, pp. 782, 790; Captain Theodore Clayton CMSR.

First Potomac Home Brigade Cavalry (Cole's)

1. Frederick H. Dyer, *A Compendium of the War of the Rebellion* (New York : 1959), Vol. III, p. 1229. All subsequent references from volume III unless otherwise noted.
2. C. Armour Newcomer, *Cole's Cavalry or Three Years in the Saddle in the Shenandoah Valley* (Baltimore, MD: 1895), pp. 31-33, 57.
3. *Baltimore Sunday News*, January 21, 1894. Transcript in the Frederick County Historical Society; Newcomer, pp. 11-18; *History and Roster*, p. 655.
4. *History and Roster* p. 655; Dyer, p.1229.

5. Newcomer, p. 19; *History and Roster* p. 656.

6. Newcomer, pp. 49-50.

7. Dyer, p. 1229; *History and Roster*, pp. 656-657; *Baltimore Sunday News*.

8. Mark M. Boatner III, *The Civil War Dictionary*, (New York: 1959), p.101; Newcomer, pp. 33-34; *History and Roster*, p. 657; Dyer, p. 1229; *OR*, Vol. 51, Part I, pp. 772, 773, 781, 782, 784.

9. Boatner, pp. 17-21.

10. *OR*, Vol. 29, Part I, p. 586; Lt. Col. George W.F. Vernon, *National Tribune*, March 30, 1894.

11. *OR*, Vol. 19, Part I, pp. 532-540; *History and Roster*, pp. 657-658; Newcomer, p. 43; Vernon, *National Tribune*, June 12, 1884; Thomas McAllister, Co. C, First Battalion, Maryland Cavalry, *National Tribune*, June 12, 1884; A slightly different version of this incident was written by Captain Thomas Bell, Eighth New York Cavalry, with emphasis on the role of his colonel. *National Tribune*, July 3, 1884.

12. Boatner, p. 814; Newcomer, p. 45; *History and Roster*, p. 658; *Baltimore Sunday News*.

13. *History and Roster*, p. 658; Dyer, p.1229.

14. Boatner, p. 937; Newcomer, p. 51; Dyer, p. 1229.

15. Newcomer, pp. 51-52; *Baltimore Sunday News*.

16. Newcomer, pp. 51-52; *History and Roster*, p. 659; *Baltimore Sunday News*.

17. Newcomer, p. 57; *OR*, Vol. 29, Part I, pp. 109-110, 144-145, 210, 642-643: Part II, p.916; *The Memoirs of Colonel John S. Mosby*, Charles W. Russell, ed., (Bloomington, IN: 1959), p. 319; Virgil C. Jones, *Gray Ghosts and Rebel Raiders*, (New York, NY: 1956), p. 204.

18. Newcomer, pp. 69-75.

19. *OR*, Vol. 29, Part I, pp. 485-492, 1010-1011; *History and Roster*, pp. 659-660; Newcomer, pp. 76-80.

20. *History and Roster*, p. 660; Newcomer, p. 86.

21. *OR*, Vol. 33, pp. 15-16, 17-18; Newcomer, pp. 93-107; Virgil C. Jones, *Ranger Mosby*, (Chapel Hill, NC: 1944), pp.164-171.

22. *OR*, Vol. 33, pp. 17-18.

23. *OR*, Vol. 33, pp.15-18; Newcomer, p. 102; *Baltimore Sunday News*; Jones, *Ranger Mosby, p. 171*.

24. Jones, *Ranger Mosby*, p. 171.

25. *OR*, Vol. 33, pp. 156, 157, 385, 386, 653, 876; *Baltimore Sunday News*; Newcomer, pp. 113, 114; *History and Roster*, p. 660; Boatner, p. 437.

26. Newcomer, pp. 113, 114; *History and Roster*, pp. 660, 661, 664.

27. Boatner, p. 588; *OR*, Vol. 37, Part I, pp. 73, 561, 562, 577, 710; Newcomer, pp. 124, 125; *History and Roster*, p. 661. The reference on page 577 of *OR*, Vol. 37 erroneously states Second Maryland Cavalry.

28. Dyer, p. 1229; Newcomer, pp. 126-127; *History and Roster*, p. 661; *OR*, Vol. 37 Part I, p, 105.

29. *History and Roster*, p. 661; Newcomer, p. 127; Boatner, p. 497.

30. Boatner, pp. 255-257; *History and Roster*, p. 661; Newcomer, p. 127; *OR*, Vol. 37, Part I, pp. 341, 690; Averill named Cole but mistakenly referred to his command as the Second Maryland Cavalry; *Baltimore Sunday News*.

31. *OR*, Vol. 37, Part II, pp. 131, 248, 704; Newcomer, pp. 131, 132.

32. *OR*, Vol. 37, Part I, p. 289; Part II, pp. 378, 392, 468, 500; Newcomer, p. 140, *History and Roster*, p. 661.

33. Newcomer, pp. 143-147; *History and Roster*, p. 661; Boatner, pp. 136, 437.
34. *OR*, Vol. 43, Part I, p. 1023: Newcomer, pp. 149-150; *History and Roster*, p. 661.
35. Boatner, pp. 743-746.
36. *OR*, Vol. 43, Part I, pp. 94, 422, 745, 986; Part II, pp. 13, 38, 486.
37. Colonel Henry A. Cole, CMSR; *OR*, Vol. 43, Part I, pp. 745, 849, 867, 890, 986; Part II, 424, 427, 736, 742, 808; Vol. 46, Part I, pp. 736, 761; Part II, pp.49, 95; *Supplement*, p.197, 224.
38. *Baltimore Sunday News*, Dyer, p. 1229; *History and Roster*, pp. 662, 663.
39. Cole, CMSR; *History and Roster*, p. 664; *Baltimore Sunday News*; *Frederick daily News*, May 26, May 28, 1909; Jacob M. Holdcroft, *Names in Stone*, (Ann Arbor, MI: 1966), Vol. I, p. 256.

Second Potomac Home Brigade Company F (Mounted)

1. *History and Roster*, p 541, 557.
2. Captain George D. Summers CMSR; *History and Roster*, p. 541.
3. *OR*, Vol. 25, Part II, pp. 34, 139, 143, 495, 501, 590,
4. *OR*, Vol. 27, Part II, p. 203; F. W. Myers, *The Comanches, A History of White's Battalion Virginia Cavalry*, (Marietta: 1956), pp. 188-190.
5. Harry Gilmor, *Four Years in the Saddle*, (Baltimore: 1987), reprint of 1866 edition with introduction by Daniel C. Toomey, pp. 92-93; *OR* Vol. 27, Part II, p. 203.
6. *OR*, Vol. 27, Part II, pp. 203-204.
7. *OR*, Vol. 29, Part II, pp. 139, 916.
8. *OR*, Vol. 29, Part II, p. 487; Gilmor, pp. 108-111; *History and Roster*, p. 542.
9. "They Are Coming!' Testimony at the Court of Inquiry on Imboden's Capture of Charles Town," Charles E. Barr, Jr. and Michael O. Musick, eds, *The Magazine of the Jefferson County Historical Society*, Vol. LIV, December 1988.
10. *OR*, Vol. 33, pp. 33-34.
11. *OR*, Vol. 33, p. 480; *History and Roster* p. 542.

Smith's Independent Company of Maryland Cavalry

1. *Supplement*, pp. 265-266.
2. *History and Roster*, p. 792; Captain George W. P. Smith CMSR; *Supplement*, p. 266.
3. *History and Roster*, p. 791; *OR*, Vol. 21, p. 964; *OR*, Vol. 25, Part II, p. 591.
4. *OR*, Vol. 29, Part II, p. 319.
5. Captain George W. P. Smith CMSR.
6. *OR*, Vol. 29, Part II, p. 612; Captain George W. P. Smith CMSR.
7. *Supplement*, p. 268.
8. *OR*, Vol. 43 Part I, p. 785.
9. Toomey, *The Civil War in Maryland*, (Baltimore: 1983), p. 139; *OR*, Vol. 43, pp. 322-323; Captain George W .P. Smith CMSR.
10. *OR*, Vol. P. 324; *Supplement*, p. 267.
11. *OR*, Vol. 46, Part III, p. 715.
12. Special Order #45 War Dept. January 28th, 1865.
13. *OR*, Vol. 46, Part III, p.542.
14. *OR*, Vol. 46, Part III, p. 1284; *History and Roster*, p.791.

Combined Bibliography

PRIMARY SOURCES

Bigelow Family Papers. Massachusetts Historical Society, Boston, MA. Reference N- 95, Box 7 ms.

Janet B. Hewett, ed. *Supplement to the Official records of the Union and Confederate Armies.* Wilmington, NC, 1996.

Matthew T. McLannahan "Civil War Record of Matthew T. McLannahan (Company I First Maryland Cavalry)." n.d./n.p. Copy in D.C.T. collection.

Maryland. "Report of the Maryland Gettysburg Monument Committee to His Excellence E. E. Jackson, Governor of Maryland June 17, 1891."

William H. Price, Private. Letter to Lewis T. Roberts February, 1863. Union Room Collection, Maryland National Guard Military Historical Society.

James E. Taylor *James E. Taylor Sketchbook.* Western Reserve Historical Society, Cleveland, OH.

United States Government. General Order No. 110 War Department, Adjutant General's Office, Washington, April 29, 1863.

United States Government. *Instructions for Field Artillery* prepared by a Board of Officers. J.P. Lippincott and Co., 1861.

United States Government, War Department. *The War of the rebellion: A Compilation of The Official Records of the Union and Confederate Armies* 128 volumes. Washington D.C., 1880 – 1901.

ARTICLES

Charles E. Barr, Jr. and Michael O. Musick eds. "They Are Coming." *The Magazine of the Jefferson County Historical Society* Volume LIV December, 1988.

Charles B. Clark "Recruitment of Union Troops in Maryland 1861 – 1865." *Maryland Historical Magazine* Volume 53 No.2 June, 1958.

Richard E. Clem "The Battle of Monocacy: One Soldiers Story." *Maryland Cracker Barrel* June, 1989.

Charles A. Earp "War Came to Town 125 Years Ago." *Towson Times* July 17, 1989.

Jack Kelbaugh "A Case of Murder." *History Notes* Volume XXVII No. 3 and 4. Published by the Ann Arrundel County Historical Society.

Daniel Carroll Toomey "Murdered – A Yankee Marylander Captain Thomas H. Watkins." *The Maryland Line* Vol. 10 No. 4 December, 1989. Published by the Montgomery County Civil War Round Table.

James H. Rigby, Captain "Three Civil War Letters of James H. Rigby by a Maryland Artillery Officer." *Maryland Historical Magazine* Volume 57, 1962.

Frank H. Schell "As an Artist Saw Antietam, A Great Raging Battlefield is Hell." *Civil War Times Illustrated* March/April 1969.

BOOKS

Allison L. Wilmer, J. H. Jarrett, and George W. W. Vernon eds. *History and Roster of Maryland Volunteers War of 1861 – 65* 2 Volumes. Baltimore, 1898. Reprint by Toomey Press 1997.

Joseph Balkoski *Beyond the Beach Head.* Harrisburg, 1989.

Joseph Balkoski *The Maryland National Guard: A History of Maryland Military Forces.* Baltimore, 1991.

John D. Billings *The History of the Tenth Massachusetts Battery of Light Artillery in the War of the Rebellion.* Boston, 1909.

Mark M. Boatner III *The Civil War Dictionary.* Baltimore, 1959.

Francis H. Brown *Harvard University in the War of 1861 – 1865.* Boston, 1886.

Jack Coggins *Arms and Equipment of the Civil War.* Garden City, NY, 1962.

Fairfax Downey *Clash of Cavalry* 3 Volumes. New York, 1959.

Frederick Dyer *A Compendium of the War of the Rebellion* 3 Volumes. New York, 1959.

Patricia L. Faust, ed. *Historical Times Illustrated Encyclopedia of the Civil War.* New York, 1986.

Harry Gilmor *Four Years in the Saddle.* New York, 1866. Butternut and Blue reprint Baltimore, 1987.

W. W. Goldsborough *The Maryland Line in the Confederate Army 1861 – 1865.* Port Washington, NY/Londoun, 1972. Second Edition.

Roger D. Hunt and Jack R. Brown *Brevet Brigadier Generals in Blue.* Gaithersburg, MD, 1990.

Laura Virginia Hale *Four Valiant Years in the Lower Shenandoah Valley 1861 – 1865.* Front Royal, VA, 1986.

Jacob M. Holdcroft *Names in Stone.* Ann Arbor, MI, 1996.

Richard B. Irwin *History of the 19th Army Corps.* New York, 1892.

Curt Johnson and Richard C. Anderson Jr. *Artillery Hell, The Employment of Artillery at Antietam.* College Station, TX, 1995.

Kent County 1628 – 1980. Chestertown, 1980.

Francis A. Lord *Civil War Collector's Encyclopedia.* Harrisburg, 1963.

Francis A. Lord *They Fought for the Union.* New York, 1960.

Henry B. McClellan *The Life and Campaigns of Major General J.E.B. Stuart.* Boston, 1885.

Massachusetts. *Massachusetts Soldiers, Sailors and Marines in the Civil War.* Compiled and published by the Adjutant General. Norwood, MA, 1932.

Massachusetts. *Vital Records of Roxbury, Massachusetts* Volume 1 Births. Salem, 1925.

Lynn R. Meekins *Men of Mark in Maryland.* Baltimore, Washington, Richmond, 1910.

Francis Trevelyn Miller ed. *The Photographic History of the Civil War* 10 volumes. New York, 1912.

The Peal Museum *Baltimore During the Civil War.* Baltimore, 1961.

F. W. Myers *The Comanches, A History of White's Battalion Virginia Cavalry.* Marietta, 1956.

George T. Ness Jr. *The Regular Army on the Eve of the Civil War.* Baltimore, 1990.

C. Armour Newcomer *Cole's Cavalry or Three Years in the Saddle in the Shenandoah Valley*. Baltimore, 1895.
Harry W. Pfanz *Gettysburg: Culps Hill and Cemetery Hill*. Chapel Hill, 1993.
Henry F. Powell *Tercentenary History of Maryland*. Chicago – Baltimore, 1925.
John Michael Priest *Antietam, the Soldiers Battle*. Shippensburg, 1989.
Davis F. Riggs *East of Gettysburg*. Bellevue, NE, 1970.
Charles W. Russell ed. *The Memoirs of Colonel John S. Mosby*. Bloomington, IN, 1959.
J. Thomas Scharf *History of Baltimore City and County* 2 Volumes. Baltimore, 1881.
J. Thomas Scharf *History of Maryland*. Baltimore, 1879. Reprint Harsboro, PA, 1967.
J. Thomas Scharf *History of Western Maryland*. Baltimore, 1882.
Scott Sumpter Sheads and Daniel Carroll Toomey *Baltimore During the Civil War*. Linthicum, MD, 1979.
Franz Sigel "Sigel on the Shenandoah Valley in 1864." *Battles and Leaders of the Civil War* 4 volumes. New York, 1884 – 1887.
Reiman Steuart *A History of the Maryland Line in the Revolutionary War 1775- 1783*. Towson, MD, 1969.
Stephen Z. Starr *The Union Cavalry in the Civil War* 3 volumes. Baton Rouge, 1979.
Paul R. Teeter *A Matter of Honor*. East Brunswick, 1982.
Daniel Carroll Toomey *The Civil War in Maryland*. Baltimore, 1983.
Daniel Carroll Toomey *Marylanders at Gettysburg*. Baltimore, 1994.
United States Navy. Naval History Department *Civil War Naval Chronology 1861 –1865*. Washington, 1971.
Lew Wallace *Lew Wallace, An Autobiography* 2 Volumes. New York, 1906.
Frederick W. Wild *Memories and History of Captain F. W. Alexander's Baltimore Battery of Light Artillery USA*. Baltimore, 1912.
Caroline E. Whitecomb, *History of the Second Massachusetts Battery (Nim's Battery) Of Artillery 1861 – 1865*. Concord, NH, no date.

CEMETERIES

Annapolis National Cemetery. "Civil War Internments at the Annapolis National Cemetery." Unpublished manuscript compiled by Jack
    Kelbaugh. Annapolis, no date.
Green Mount, Baltimore, MD. Cemetery records.
Old National, Baltimore, MD. Grave stones.

NEWSPAPERS

Baltimore *American Commercial Advertizer*   Baltimore *Sun*   Baltimore *Sunday News*
Baltimore *News Post*   *National Tribune*   Frederick *Daily News*

INSTITUTIONS AND PUBLIC DOCUMENTS

Antietam National Battlefield Park, Sharpsburg, MD
    "Artillery at Antietam." National Park Service Publication n.d./n.p.
    Position markers on the battlefield.
    Cope time and position maps.
    Lt. Theodore Vanneman's letter of September 13, 1862.
Cecil County Historical Society
    Cecil Democrat
    Cecil Whig
    Morton F. Taylor "Sketch of Snow's Battery." Typescript, no date.
Maryland Historical Society, Baltimore, MD.
    Frederic A. Alexander, "Battery Maneuvers by Bugle." Pamphlet #653.
    Baltimore City Directory, 1865 –66.
    John L. Blecker "Biography of John Henry Alexander" ms, Diehlam-Hayward Genealogy File.
    "Soldiers Buried in Green Mount Cemetery" ms, Vertical File 28, Filing Case A.
Maryland State Archives, Annapolis, MD.
    Election of Officers, Eagle Battery, June 4, 1863; Junior Battery, July 7, 1865, ms.
    Muster Rolls, First Maryland Heavy Artillery, ms.
    Muster Rolls, Battery D, First Maryland Light Artillery, ms.
    Civil War flag collection #1650 –27.
National Archives, Washington, DC.
    Microfilm Search Room:
        Compiled Military Services Records of Soldiers Who Served in Organizations from the State of Maryland, MicroCopy NR. M384.
        Index to Pension Records, MicroCopy Nr. T288
        Register of Enlistments in the Regular Army, micro Copy Nr. M233.
    Military Reference Branch (NNRM) Textual Reference Division
    Record Group, Records of the Adjutant General's Office, Volunteer Service Division Files.
    Case of Captain John M. Bruce, Battery D, First Maryland Light Artillery, ms.
    Special Order Books (bound volumes)
    Regimental Records: Morning Reports, Order Book, ms.

INDEX

District of Delaware, 135.
District of West Florida and Southern Alabama, 118.
Dix, Col. John A., 18, 19, 21, 38, 39, 121, 122.
Doubleday, Gen. Abner, 26, 27.
Draft 2, 3.
Drake, Maj. George B. 117.
Drummandtown, VA, 18, 122, 135, 156.
Duncan, Sgt. Andrew, 122.
Duncan, Lt. David, 69.
Duvall, Capt. Robert E., 121, 122, 125, 127.
Dysche, Capt. Lewis, 151.

E
Early, Jubal A., 50, 147.
Eastville, VA, 18, 122, 127.
Edwards Ferry, 99, 139.
Embery, Sgt. Charles U., 99.
Emmittsburg, MD, 101, 138.
Ensel, Pvt. Wilber M., 115.
Ewell, Gen. Richard S., 46, 152.
Evans, Col. Andrea W., 103, 105.

F
Fearong, 1st Sgt. Joseph T., 159.
Fells Point Eagle Artillery, 67.
Five Forks, VA, Battle of, 105.
Firey, Capt. William, 138.
Fitzhough, Captain, 125.
Flory, Maj. Alexander M., 145, 148.
Fort Delaware, 72.
Fort Dix, 132.
Fort Gains, 118, 120.
Fort Hell, 104.
Fort McHenry, 43, 53, 66, 69, 129.
Fort Marshall, 66, 67.
Fort Morgan, 118.
Fort Number One, 66.
Fort C.F. Smith, 59
Fort Tillinghast, 59.
Fort Worthington, 66
Foy, Sgt. James C., 125.
Frazier, John Jr., 114.
Frederick City, MD 50, 94, 99, 100, 139, 140, 142, 145.
Fredericksburg, Battle of, 37, 88, 96.
Front Royal, VA, 94, 152.
Fuget, Cpl. George, 108.

G
Gallagher, Capt. Frank, 142.
Gallion, Lt. Aquilla S., 154.
Galvanized Yankees, 102.
Geary, Gen. John W., 961.
Gerry, Lt. Lucius A., 35, 36, 40.
Gettysburg, Battle of, 2, 29, 30, 89, 90, 102, 126.
Geyer, Pvt. John, 105.
Gilmor, Maj. Harry, 152.
Glunt, Sgt. Henry, 93.
Grant, Ulysses S., 90, 104, 105.
Green, Pvt. Charles, 54.
Green, Lt. Hanson, 140.
Green Mount Cemetery, 19, 56.
Gregg, Gen. Davis McM., 96, 98.

Grinder, Capt. Eli D., 115.
Grinell, Lt., 108.

H
Haight, Lt. Francis R., 114.
Halleck, Gen. Henry W., 122, 144.
Harper's Ferry, WV, 31, 46, 48, 54, 92-94, 125, 135, 137, 153.
Harvey, Sgt. John H., 70.
Hatch, Gen. Edward, 93.
Hayes, Gen. Rutherford B., 42.
Herbert, Lt. Gideon, 127.
Herbert, Sgt. Thomas R., 125.
Hicks, Thomas H., 1, 4, 29.
Hitescheu, Lt. Daniel, 95.
Hitescheu, Sgt. Phillip, 95.
Hoffer, Pvt. Henry, 108.
Hooker, Gen. Joseph, 27, 38, 88, 96, 98, 159.
Harding, Sgt. John S., 116
Harding, Pvt. Edward S., 116.
Horner, Maj. John, 138, 142, 154.
Houghs, Sgt, Thomas, 94.
Hunt, Gen. Henry J., 19, 34.
Hunter, Capt. Albert, 141.
Hunter, Gen. David, 41, 42, 145.
Howe, Gen. Albion P., 29.
Hyde, Maj. Thomas W., 25.

I, J
Irwin, Col. William H., 25.
Jackson, Pvt. Henry, 44.
Jackson, Gen. Thomas, 93.
Jarbo, Pvt. William, 108.
Jenkins, Lt. John H., 69.
Jones, Gen. William E., 41.
Jordon, Pvt., Jim, 101.
Jude, Maj. Henry B., 135.

K
Kause, Spphia, 119.
Kaxtz, Gen. August V., 103, 104.
Keedysville, MD, 147.
Kelly, Pvt. Ervine, 108.
Kenly, Gen. John R., 46, 67, 68, 72, 95, 136, 159.
Kentucky, First Artillery, 42.
Kesley, Maj. William, 113.
Kid, Lt. James H., 35, 36, 42.
Kimble, Lt. Robert J., 99.
Kirby, Lt. Co. Byron, 114, 117, 120.
Klinke, Cpl. John C., 115.
Knight, Lt. Col., 158.
Kraft, Capt. John W., 73.
Kreager, Capt. Francis M., 99.

L
Leary, Lt. Peter Jr., 46, 47, 50, 51, 56.
Libby Prison, 49.
Link, Capt. Daniel, 141.
Lockwood, Gen. Henry, 18-20, 57, 58, 103, 121, 132, 153, 153.
Louden Park Cemetery, 43.
Loudon Heights, Va., 143, 147.
Louisiana Military Organizations:
    Cavalry: 9th Bat.115; 10th Bat. 115.